ORGANIC COO

FF

Ren
by in
in per
by ph

ORGANIC COOKING

150 DELICIOUSLY HEALTHY RECIPES SHOWN IN 250 PHOTOGRAPHS

YSANNE SPEVACK

southwater

This edition is published by Southwater,
an imprint of Anness Publishing Ltd, Blaby Road,
Wigston, Leicestershire LE18 4SE; info@anness.com

www.southwaterbooks.com; www.annesspublishing.com

If you like the images in this book and would like to
investigate using them for publishing, promotions or
advertising, please visit www.practicalpictures.com
for more information.

© Anness Publishing Ltd 2012

Publisher: Joanna Lorenz
Senior Managing Editor: Conor Kilgallon
Project Editor: Brian Burns
Recipes: Ysanne Spevack
Photography: Peter Anderson and Simon Smith
Home Economist: Annabel Ford
Stylist: Helen Trent
Designer: Nigel Partridge
Production Controller: Steve Lang

NOTES

Bracketed terms are intended for American readers.
For all recipes, quantities are given in both metric and
imperial measures and, where appropriate, in standard
cups and spoons. Follow one set of measures, but not
a mixture, because they are not interchangeable.
Standard spoon and cup measures are level. 1 tsp = 5ml,
1 tbsp = 15ml, 1 cup = 250ml/8fl oz.
Australian standard tablespoons are 20ml. Australian
readers should use 3 tsp in place of 1 tbsp for measuring
small quantities.
American pints are 16fl oz/2 cups. American readers
should use 20fl oz/2.5 cups in place of 1 pint when
measuring liquids.
Electric oven temperatures in this book are for
conventional ovens. When using a fan oven, the
temperature will probably need to be reduced by about
10–20°C/20–40°F. Since ovens vary, you should check
with your manufacturer's instruction book for guidance.
The nutritional analysis given for each recipe is calculated
per portion (i.e. serving or item), unless otherwise stated.
If the recipe gives a range, such as Serves 4–6, then the
nutritional analysis will be for the smaller portion size,
i.e. 6 servings. The analysis does not include optional
ingredients, such as salt added to taste.
Medium (US large) eggs are used unless otherwise stated.
Front cover shows roasted shallot and squash salad
– for recipe, see page 101.

PUBLISHER'S NOTE

Contents

Introduction

Interest in organic food and farming is at an all-time high. As we become more aware of the effects of pesticides and chemicals on the environment and in our diets, the more we are turning to organic food for flavour, taste, nutrition and natural good health. Put simply, we choose organic food because we appreciate good food and a better way of living.

Food for health

Organic meat, poultry and dairy produce are of excellent quality and more nutritious than intensively farmed produce. Organic fruit and vegetables are full of juice and flavour, and there are many unusual varieties to try. Organic fruit and vegetables ripen more naturally in richer soil, obtaining the maximum variety of micronutrients.

As part of their defence against pests, fruits and vegetables contain phytonutrients, which also help to fight disease and promote good health in people. In contrast, agrochemical plants are liberally sprayed with nitrogen fertilizers to promote faster growth. A side effect is that the plants produce fewer and less diverse phytonutrients. Organic crops are grown in more balanced, less nitrogen-rich soil.

There is also evidence that people who eat organic food build up a stronger immunity to disease than those who consistently eat food laden with chemicals. Other benefits include fewer flus, colds and catarrhal problems, clear skin, improved dental health and general vitality, and, some studies suggest, increased fertility.

Organic food is free from hydrogenated fats, which are a major contributor to obesity, heart disease and cancer. Also, organic meat generally contains less saturated fat than non-organic, and it is easier to remove as it is less evenly distributed.

Meat, poultry, eggs and milk derived from grass-fed animals contain more conjugated linoleic acid (CLA), which can help maintain a healthy weight and reduce the risk of heart disease and cancer.

A matter of taste

Of course, there is another very good reason to go organic: organic food tastes better than intensively farmed produce, and for very good reasons.

While most agrochemical crops are bred for their high yield, organic produce is grown from seeds bred

LEFT: *The freshest organic produce makes all the difference to this marinated avocado and salmon salad.*

ABOVE: *Provençal aioli with smoked haddock is fresh, tasty and filling.*

ABOVE: *Sizzling hot skewered chicken is an ideal dish for the barbecue.*

ABOVE: *Chocolate mousse with glazed kumquats is a sumptuous combination.*

primarily for flavour. Many organic farmers also cultivate heirloom crops – crops once highly prized but no longer considered profitable. Organic growers in industrialized nations produce about a hundred different kinds of potato, compared to the 20 or so agrochemical varieties on sale in the USA or UK.

Organic crops are grown more slowly to allow flavour to develop naturally, while the higher quantities of phytonutrients also add flavour. Sugar levels are often slightly higher in organic produce, particularly carrots and apples. Organic fruit, which ripens naturally, is sweeter and more flavoursome. Having less water also intensifies the flavours of organic fruits and vegetables.

As with crops, organic farmers are increasingly breeding animals noted for their taste rather than their yield. Slow rearing methods further enhance the flavour of the meats produced.

Organic prepared foods also contain very few of the chemical flavourings and flavour enhancers found in non-organic foods. They taste so good that they don't need them.

Following the seasons, from spring through summer and autumn to winter, the recipes in this book work with the ingredients naturally available for the time of year to give you fresh, flavoursome, deeply satisfying meals time after time. "The organic kitchen" section is packed with useful

information on everything you need to know about fruit, vegetables, fish, meat, dairy, grains, bread, pasta and more. Before long, not only will you be heading for the organic section in your local supermarket, you'll find yourself investigating box schemes, farmers' markets and all manner of small, local organic suppliers.

Ultimately, organic food is that rarest of fine pleasures – something that tastes good and does you good. It is also, as the stunning range of recipes in this book proves, rich in variety, from the hearty and rustic to the elegant and exquisite – a menu for all tastes, from vegetarians to fish lovers and meat eaters. Get cooking.

Spring

As the days get a little longer and the weather warmer, fresh organic ingredients, such as tender, brightly coloured young vegetables and new season lamb, start to appear in the shops and farmers' markets. Light fish dishes are also a popular choice now after long, dark winter days. For dessert, nothing tastes better than tender spring rhubarb, either served with ginger ice cream or made into a meringue pie.

Parsley and rocket salad

This salad is light but full of flavour, and makes a tasty first course, ideal for a spring dinner party. Shavings of rich-tasting cheese ensure that this salad is special.

SERVES 6 (FIRST COURSE)

1 garlic clove, halved
115g/4oz good white bread, cut into
    1cm/½ in thick slices
45ml/3 tbsp olive oil, plus extra for
    shallow frying
75g/3oz rocket (arugula) leaves
75g/3oz baby spinach
25g/1oz flat leaf parsley, leaves only
45ml/3 tbsp salted capers, rinsed and dried
40g/1½oz Parmesan cheese or premium
    Italian-style vegetarian cheese,
    pared into shavings

FOR THE DRESSING

25ml/1½ tbsp black olive paste
1 garlic clove, finely chopped
5ml/1 tsp smooth organic mustard
75ml/5 tbsp olive oil
10ml/2 tsp balsamic vinegar
ground black pepper

1 First make the dressing. Whisk the black olive paste, garlic and mustard together in a mixing bowl. Gradually whisk in the olive oil, then the vinegar. Adjust the seasoning to taste with black pepper – the dressing should not need any additional salt.

2 Heat the oven to 190°C/375°F/ Gas 5. Rub the halved garlic clove over the bread and tear the slices into bitesize croûtons. Toss them in the olive oil and place on a small baking tray. Bake in the oven for 10 –15 minutes, stirring once, until golden brown. Cool on kitchen paper.

3 Mix the rocket, baby spinach and flat leaf parsley together in a large salad bowl.

4 Heat a shallow layer of olive oil in a frying pan. Add the capers and fry briefly until crisp. Scoop out straight away and drain on kitchen paper.

5 Toss the dressing and croûtons into the salad and divide it among six individual bowls or plates.

6 Scatter the cheese shavings and the fried capers over the top of the salad and serve immediately.

Nutritional information per portion: Energy 219kcal/909kJ; Protein 5.1g; Carbohydrate 10g, of which sugars 1g; Fat 17.9g, of which saturates 3.6g; Cholesterol 7mg; Calcium 155mg; Fibre 1.1g; Sodium 303mg.

Asparagus with lemon sauce

This is a good spring dish as the asparagus gives the immune system a kick-start to help detoxify after winter. The sauce has a light, fresh taste and brings out the best in the asparagus.

SERVES 4 (FIRST COURSE)

675g/1¹/₂lb asparagus, tough ends removed, and tied in a bundle
15ml/1 tbsp cornflour (cornstarch)
10ml/2 tsp unrefined sugar or rapadura
2 egg yolks
juice of 1¹/₂ lemons
sea salt

1 Cook the asparagus in boiling salted water for 7–10 minutes. Drain well (reserving 200ml/7fl oz/scant 1 cup of the cooking liquid) and arrange in a serving dish. Set aside.

2 Blend the cornflour with the cooled, reserved liquid and place in a small pan. Bring to the boil, stirring constantly with a wooden spoon, then cook gently until the sauce thickens slightly. Stir in the sugar, then remove from the heat and allow to cool slightly.

3 Beat the egg yolks thoroughly with the lemon juice and stir gradually into the cooled sauce.

4 Cook the sauce over a very low heat, stirring all the time, until it thickens. Be careful not to overheat the sauce or it may curdle.

5 Once the sauce has thickened, remove the pan from the heat and continue stirring for 1 minute.

6 Season with salt or sugar if necessary, then allow the sauce to cool slightly.

7 Stir the cooled lemon sauce, then pour a little over the asparagus. Cover and chill for at least 2 hours before serving accompanied by the rest of the lemon sauce.

Nutritional information per portion: Energy 96kcal/399kJ; Protein 6.4g; Carbohydrate 9.4g, of which sugars 5.8g; Fat 3.8g, of which saturates 1g; Cholesterol 101mg; Calcium 59mg; Fibre 2.9g; Sodium 8mg.

Assorted seaweed salad

This salad is a fine example of the traditional Japanese idea of eating: look after your appetite and your health at the same time. Seaweed is a nutritious, alkaline food that is rich in fibre. Its unusual flavours are a great complement to fish and tofu dishes.

SERVES 4

5g/¹/₈oz each dried wakame, dried arame
    and dried hijiki seaweeds
about 130g/4¹/₂oz enokitake mushrooms
2 spring onions (scallions)
a few ice cubes
¹/₂ cucumber, cut lengthways
250g/9oz mixed salad leaves

FOR THE MARINADE
15ml/1 tbsp rice vinegar
6.5ml/1¹/₄ tsp salt

FOR THE DRESSING
60ml/4 tbsp rice vinegar
7.5ml/1¹/₂ tsp toasted sesame oil
15ml/1 tbsp shoyu
15ml/1 tbsp water with a pinch of
    dashi-no-moto (dashi stock granules)
2.5cm/1in piece fresh root ginger,
    finely grated

1 First rehydrate the seaweeds. Soak the dried wakame seaweed for 10 minutes in one bowl of water and, in a separate bowl of water, soak the dried arame and hijiki seaweeds together for 30 minutes.

2 Trim the hard end of the enokitake mushroom stalks, then cut the bunch in half and separate the stems.

3 Slice the spring onions into thin, 4cm/1¹/₂in long strips, then soak the strips in a bowl of cold water with a few ice cubes added to make them curl up. Drain. Slice the cucumber into thin, half-moon shapes.

4 Cook the wakame and enokitake in boiling water for 2 minutes, then add the arame and hijiki for a few seconds. Immediately remove from the heat. Drain and sprinkle over the vinegar and salt while still warm. Chill until needed.

5 Mix the dressing ingredients in a bowl. Arrange the mixed salad leaves in a large bowl with the cucumber on top, then add the seaweed and enokitake mixture. Decorate the salad with spring onion curls and serve with the dressing.

Nutritional information per portion: Energy 26kcal/107kJ; Protein 1.5g; Carbohydrate 2.1g, of which sugars 2g; Fat 1.3g, of which saturates 0.2g; Cholesterol 0mg; Calcium 28mg; Fibre 1.2g; Sodium 272mg.

Beetroot and red onion salad

There is a wide variety of organic beetroots available – this salad looks especially attractive when made with a mixture of red and yellow. Try it with rich meats such as roast beef or cooked ham.

SERVES 6

500g/1¼lb small red and yellow
    beetroot (beet)
75ml/5 tbsp water
60ml/4 tbsp olive oil
90g/3½oz/scant 1 cup walnut or
    pecan halves
5ml/1 tsp unrefined caster (superfine)
    sugar or rapadura, plus a little extra
    for the dressing
30ml/2 tbsp walnut oil
15ml/1 tbsp balsamic vinegar
5ml/1 tsp soy sauce
5ml/1 tsp grated orange rind
2.5ml/½ tsp ground roasted
    coriander seeds
5–10ml/1–2 tsp orange juice
1 red onion, halved and very thinly sliced
15–30ml/1–2 tbsp chopped
    fresh fennel
75g/3oz watercress or mizuna leaves
handful of baby red chard or beetroot
    (beet) leaves (optional)
sea salt and ground black pepper

1 Heat the oven to 180°C/350°F/ Gas 4. Place a single layer of beetroot in a shallow ovenproof dish and add the water. Cover tightly with a close-fitting lid or foil and bake for 1–1½ hours.

2 Allow to cool. Peel, then slice into strips and toss with 15ml/1 tbsp of olive oil. Leave aside in a large bowl.

3 Heat 15ml/1 tbsp of olive oil in a small frying pan and cook the walnuts or pecans until they begin to brown. Add the sugar and cook, stirring, until the nuts begin to caramelize. Season with 2.5ml/ ½ tsp salt and lots of ground black pepper. Leave to cool on a plate.

4 In a jug (pitcher) or small bowl, whisk together the remaining olive oil, the walnut oil, vinegar, soy sauce, orange rind and ground roasted coriander seeds to make the dressing. Season with salt and pepper to taste and add a pinch of caster sugar. Whisk in orange juice to taste.

5 Separate the red onion slices into half-rings and add them to the slices or strips of beetroot. Add the dressing and toss thoroughly to mix.

6 To serve, toss the salad with the fennel, watercress or mizuna and red chard or beetroot leaves (if using). Put in individual bowls or plates and sprinkle with the caramelized nuts.

Nutritional information per portion: Energy 239kcal/991kJ; Protein 3.3g; Carbohydrate 8.2g, of which sugars 7.2g; Fat 21.7g, of which saturates 2.3g; Cholesterol 0mg; Calcium 50mg; Fibre 2.6g; Sodium 121mg.

Garganelli with spring vegetables

Fresh, brightly coloured organic spring vegetables are great served with pasta. A light sauce of dry white wine, extra virgin olive oil and fresh herbs marry the two together for a delicious flavour.

SERVES 4

1 bunch asparagus, about 350g/12oz
4 young carrots
1 bunch spring onions (scallions)
130g/4¹⁄₂oz shelled fresh peas
350g/12oz/3 cups dried garganelli
60ml/4 tbsp dry white wine
90ml/6 tbsp extra virgin olive oil
a few sprigs fresh flat leaf parsley, mint
    and basil, leaves stripped and chopped
sea salt and ground black pepper
freshly grated Parmesan cheese or
    premium Italian-style vegetarian
    cheese, to serve

1 Trim off and discard the woody part of the asparagus stems. Cut off the tips on the diagonal. Cut the stems diagonally into 4cm/1¹⁄₂in pieces. Cut the carrots and spring onions diagonally into similar-size pieces.

2 Put the carrots, peas, asparagus stems and tips into a large pan of salted boiling water. Bring back to the boil. Reduce the heat and simmer for 8–10 minutes, until tender.

3 Meanwhile, cook the pasta in salted boiling water for 10–12 minutes, until just tender.

4 Drain the asparagus, carrots and peas and return to the pan. Add the white wine, olive oil and salt and black pepper to taste, then gently toss over a medium to high heat until the wine has reduced and the vegetables glisten with the olive oil.

5 Drain the garganelli and tip it into a large warmed bowl. Add the vegetables, spring onions and sprigs of fresh herbs and toss together well. Then divide the pasta among four warmed individual plates and serve immediately, with freshly grated cheese.

Nutritional information per portion: Energy 738kcal/3092kJ; Protein 29.5g; Carbohydrate 74g, of which sugars 5.2g; Fat 38.1g, of which saturates 10.4g; Cholesterol 38mg; Calcium 492mg; Fibre 4.3g; Sodium 416mg.

Marinated salmon with avocado salad

Use only the freshest organic salmon for this salad. The marinade of lemon juice and dashi-konbu "cooks" the salmon, which is then served with avocado, toasted almonds and salad leaves.

SERVES 4

2 very fresh salmon tails, skinned and
    filleted, 250g/9oz total weight
juice of 1 lemon
10cm/4in dashi-konbu seaweed, wiped with a
    damp cloth and cut into 4 strips
1 ripe avocado
4 shiso or basil leaves, stalks removed and
    cut in half lengthways

about 115g/4oz mixed leaves such as lamb's
    lettuce, frisée or rocket (arugula)
45ml/3 tbsp flaked (sliced) almonds, toasted
    in a dry frying pan until slightly browned

FOR THE MISO MAYONNAISE
90ml/6 tbsp good-quality mayonnaise
15ml/1 tbsp miso paste
ground black pepper

1 Cut the first salmon fillet in half crossways at the tail end where the fillet is not wider than 4cm/1½in. Cut the wider part in half lengthways. Cut the other fillet in the same way.

2 Pour the lemon juice into a wide, shallow plastic container and add two of the dashi-konbu pieces. Lay the salmon fillets on the base and sprinkle with the rest of the dashi-konbu. Marinate for 15 minutes. Turn the salmon and leave for another 15 minutes. It should now be pink. Remove from the marinade and wipe with kitchen paper.

3 With a sharp knife at an angle, cut the salmon into 5mm/¼in thick slices against the grain. Halve the avocado and sprinkle with salmon marinade. Remove the avocado stone (pit) and skin. Slice to the same thickness as the salmon.

4 Mix the miso mayonnaise ingredients in a bowl. Spread 5ml/1 tsp on to the back of each shiso or basil leaf. Mix the rest with 15ml/1 tbsp of the remaining marinade to loosen the mayonnaise.

5 Arrange the salad leaves on four plates. Add the avocado, salmon, shiso leaves and almonds and toss lightly. Drizzle over the remaining mayonnaise and serve immediately.

Nutritional information per portion: Energy 432kcal/1787kJ; Protein 16.2g, Carbohydrate 2.3g, of which sugars 1.4g; Fat 39.8g, of which saturates 6.2g; Cholesterol 48mg; Calcium 54mg; Fibre 2.3g; Sodium 134mg.

Tapenade with quail's eggs and crudités

This olive-based spread or dip makes a sociable start to a meal. Serve the tapenade with hard-boiled quail's eggs or small organic hen's eggs and a selection of mixed spring vegetable crudités.

SERVES 6

225g/8oz/2 cups pitted black olives
2 large garlic cloves, peeled
15ml/1 tbsp salted capers, rinsed
6 canned or bottled anchovy fillets
50g/2oz good-quality canned tuna
5–10ml/1–2 tsp cognac (optional)
5ml/1 tsp chopped fresh thyme
30ml/2 tbsp chopped fresh parsley
30–60ml/2–4 tbsp extra virgin olive oil
a dash of lemon juice
30ml/2 tbsp crème fraîche or fromage
   frais (optional)
12–18 quail's eggs
ground black pepper

FOR THE CRUDITÉS
spring onions (scallions), halved if large
bunch of radishes, trimmed
bunch of baby fennel, trimmed and
   halved if large, or 1 large fennel bulb,
   cut into thin wedges

1 Process the olives, garlic cloves, capers, drained anchovies and tuna in a food processor or blender. Transfer to a mixing bowl and stir in the cognac, if using, the thyme, parsley and enough olive oil to make a paste. Season to taste with pepper and a dash of lemon juice. Stir in the crème fraîche or fromage frais, if using, and transfer to a serving bowl.

2 Place the quail's eggs in a pan of cold water and bring to the boil. Cook for only 2 minutes, then immediately drain and plunge the eggs into iced water to stop them from cooking any further and to make them easier to shell.

3 When the eggs are cold, carefully part-shell them.

4 Serve the tapenade with the eggs and crudités and offer French bread, unsalted butter or oil and sea salt to accompany them.

Nutritional information per portion: Energy 157kcal/665kJ; Protein 6.3g; Carbohydrate 28.4g, of which sugars 1.8g; Fat 2.8g, of which saturates 0.6g; Cholesterol 37mg; Calcium 76mg; Fibre 1.5g; Sodium 522mg.

Oysters Rockefeller

This is the perfect dish for those who prefer their oysters lightly cooked. As a cheaper alternative, give mussels or clams the same treatment – they will also taste delicious.

SERVES 6

450g/1lb/3 cups coarse sea salt, plus
    extra to serve
24 oysters, opened
115g/4oz/¹⁄₂ cup butter or
    non-hydrogenated margarine
2 shallots, finely chopped
500g/1¹⁄₄lb spinach leaves,
    finely chopped
60ml/4 tbsp chopped fresh parsley
60ml/4 tbsp chopped celery leaves
90ml/6 tbsp fresh white or wholemeal
    (whole-wheat) breadcrumbs
cayenne pepper
sea salt and ground black pepper
10–20ml/2–4 tsp vodka
lemon wedges, to serve

1 Preheat the oven to 220°C/425°F/Gas 7. Make a bed of coarse salt on two large baking sheets. Set the oysters in the half-shell in the bed of salt to keep them steady. Set aside.

2 Melt the butter or margarine in a frying pan. Add the chopped shallots and cook them over a low heat for 2–3 minutes until they are softened. Stir in the spinach and let it wilt.

3 Add the parsley, celery leaves and breadcrumbs to the pan and fry gently for 5 minutes. Season with salt, pepper and cayenne pepper.

4 Divide the stuffing among the oysters. Drizzle a few drops of vodka over each oyster, then bake for about 5 minutes until bubbling and golden brown. Serve on a heated platter on a shallow salt bed with lemon wedges.

Nutritional information per portion: Energy 210kcal/867kJ; Protein 6.4g; Carbohydrate 3.4g, of which sugars 2.1g; Fat 17g, of which saturates 10.1g; Cholesterol 60mg; Calcium 211mg; Fibre 2.3g; Sodium 406mg.

Leek and mussel tartlets

Wild mussels can simply be gathered off rocks in shallow water by hand. Serve these vividly coloured tarts as a first course, with a few salad leaves, such as watercress, rocket and frisée.

SERVES 6

large pinch of saffron threads
2 large leeks, sliced
30ml/2 tbsp olive oil
2 large yellow (bell) peppers, halved,
    seeded, grilled (broiled), peeled and cut
    into strips
900g/2lb mussels
2 large eggs
300ml/¹/₂ pint/1¹/₄ cups single (light)
    cream or soya cream

30ml/2 tbsp finely chopped fresh parsley
sea salt and ground black pepper
salad leaves, to serve

FOR THE PASTRY
225g/8oz/2 cups plain (all-purpose) flour
115g/4oz/¹/₂ cup chilled butter, diced
45–60ml/3–4 tbsp chilled water

1 To make the pastry, sift the flour into a mixing bowl, then rub the butter in with your fingertips until the mixture resembles fine breadcrumbs. Sprinkle with 45ml/3 tbsp of water and mix with a round-bladed knife to form a soft dough. Wrap it in clear film (plastic wrap) and chill for 30 minutes.

2 Heat the oven to 190°C/375°F/Gas 5. Roll out the pastry and line six 10cm/4in tartlet tins (muffin pans). Prick the bases and line the sides with foil. Bake for 10 minutes. Remove the foil and bake for 5–8 minutes. Reduce the temperature to 180°C/350°F/Gas 4.

3 Soak the saffron in 15ml/1 tbsp hot water for 10 minutes. Pan fry the leeks in oil over a medium heat for 6–8 minutes. Add the peppers and cook for 2 minutes.

4 In a large pan, add 10ml/2 tsp salt to 2.5cm/1in depth of boiling water. Scrub the mussels and remove the beards. Discard any that stay open when tapped and use the rest. Cover and cook over a high heat for 3–4 minutes, or until the mussels open. Discard any unopened mussels. Shell the remainder.

5 Beat the eggs, cream and saffron liquid together. Season with salt and pepper and whisk in the parsley. Arrange the leeks, peppers and mussels in the cases, add the egg mixture and bake for 20–25 minutes. Serve with salad leaves.

Nutritional information per portion: Energy 506kcal/2112kJ; Protein 17.2g; Carbohydrate 35.1g, of which sugars 6.1g; Fat 34.1g, of which saturates 18.3g; Cholesterol 155mg; Calcium 221mg; Fibre 2.8g; Sodium 273mg.

Pasta and chickpea soup

A simple, country-style soup. The shapes of the pasta and the beans complement one another beautifully. Look out for really large pasta shells in farmers' markets and good organic stores.

SERVES 4–6

1 onion
2 carrots
2 celery sticks
60ml/4 tbsp olive oil
400g/14oz can chickpeas, rinsed
   and drained
200g/7oz can cannellini beans, rinsed
   and drained
150ml/1/4 pint/2/3 cup passata (bottled
   strained tomatoes)
120ml/4fl oz/1/2 cup water
1.5 litres/21/2 pints/61/4 cups
   chicken stock
2 fresh or dried rosemary sprigs
200g/7oz dried giant conchiglie
sea salt and ground black pepper
freshly grated Parmesan cheese or
   premium Italian-style vegetarian
   cheese, to serve

1 Finely chop the onion, carrots and celery sticks. Heat the olive oil in a large pan, add the chopped vegetable mixture and cook over a low heat, stirring frequently, for 5 minutes, or until the vegetables are just beginning to soften.

2 Add the chickpeas and cannellini beans, stir well to mix, then cook for 5 minutes. Stir in the passata and water, then cook, stirring, for 2–3 minutes.

3 Add 475ml/16fl oz/2 cups of the stock and one of the rosemary sprigs. Bring to the boil, cover, then simmer gently, stirring occasionally, for 1 hour.

4 Pour in the remaining stock, add the pasta and bring to the boil, stirring. Lower the heat slightly and simmer, stirring frequently, until the pasta is *al dente*: 7–8 minutes or according to the instructions on the packet.

5 When the pasta is cooked, taste the soup for seasoning. Remove the rosemary and serve the soup hot in warmed bowls, topped with grated cheese and a few rosemary leaves from the rosemary sprig.

Nutritional information per portion: Energy 454kcal/1916kJ; Protein 17.3g; Carbohydrate 66.3g, of which sugars 7.7g; Fat 15.2g, of which saturates 2.1g; Cholesterol 0mg; Calcium 105mg; Fibre 9.7g; Sodium 510mg.

Chicken, avocado and spring onion soup

Organic avocados ripen naturally over a longer period of time than non-organic, producing really rich-flavoured fruit. Here, they add a creaminess to this delicious soup.

SERVES 6

1.5 litres/2¹/2 pints/6¹/4 cups
   chicken stock
¹/2 fresh chilli, seeded
2 skinless, boneless chicken breast fillets
1 avocado
4 spring onions (scallions), finely sliced
400g/14oz can chickpeas, drained
sea salt and freshly ground black pepper

1 Pour the chicken stock into a large pan and add the chilli. Bring to the boil, add the whole chicken breast fillets, then lower the heat and simmer for about 10 minutes, or until the chicken is cooked.

2 Remove the pan from the heat and lift out the chicken breasts with a slotted spoon. Leave to cool a little, then, using two forks, shred the chicken into small pieces. Set the shredded chicken aside.

3 Pour the chicken stock into a food processor or blender. Process the mixture until smooth, then return to the pan.

4 Cut the avocado in half, remove the skin and stone (pit), then slice the flesh into 2cm/³/4in pieces. Add it to the stock, with the spring onions and chickpeas.

5 Return the shredded chicken to the pan, with salt and pepper to taste. Heat gently, then spoon into warmed bowls and serve.

Nutritional information per portion: Energy 163kcal/686kJ; Protein 17.3g; Carbohydrate 11.3g, of which sugars 0.5g; Fat 5.7g, of which saturates 1g; Cholesterol 35mg; Calcium 36mg; Fibre 3.4g; Sodium 178mg.

Fillets of sea bream in filo pastry

Any firm fish fillets can be used for this dish, such as bass, grouper, red mullet and snapper. As the number of organic seawater fish farms grows, an increasing variety of breeds is becoming available.

SERVES 4

8 small waxy salad potatoes,
    preferably red-skinned
200g/7oz sorrel, stalks removed
30ml/2 tbsp olive oil
16 filo pastry sheets, thawed if frozen
4 sea bream fillets, about 175g/6oz each,
    scaled but not skinned

50g/2oz/¹/₄ cup butter, melted or
    60ml/4 tbsp olive oil
120ml/4fl oz/¹/₂ cup fish stock
250ml/8fl oz/1 cup whipping cream or
    soya cream
sea salt and ground black pepper
finely diced red (bell) pepper and salad
    leaves, to garnish

1 Preheat the oven to 200°C/400°F/Gas 6. Cook the potatoes in a pan of lightly salted boiling water for about 20 minutes, or until just tender. Drain and leave to cool.

2 Set about half the sorrel leaves aside. Shred the remaining leaves by piling up six or eight at a time, rolling them up like a fat cigar and slicing them.

3 Thinly slice the potatoes lengthways. Brush a baking sheet with a little oil. Lay a sheet of filo pastry on the sheet; brush with oil. Lay a second sheet crossways over it. Repeat with two more sheets. Arrange a quarter of the sliced potatoes in the centre, season and add a quarter of the shredded sorrel. Lay a bream fillet on top, skin-side up. Season.

4 Loosely fold the filo pastry up and over to make a neat parcel. Make three more parcels; place on the baking sheet. Brush with half the melted butter or oil. Bake for about 20 minutes until the filo is puffed up and golden brown.

5 To make the sorrel sauce, heat the remaining butter or oil in a pan, add the reserved sorrel and cook gently for 3 minutes, stirring, until it wilts. Stir in the stock and cream. Heat almost to boiling point, stirring so that the sorrel breaks down. Season to taste and keep hot until the fish parcels are ready. Serve garnished with red pepper and salad leaves. Hand round the sauce separately.

Nutritional information per portion: Energy 651kcal/2710kJ; Protein 35.8g; Carbohydrate 23.2g, of which sugars 3.3g; Fat 46.8g, of which saturates 23.2g; Cholesterol 159mg; Calcium 222mg; Fibre 2g; Sodium 359mg.

Seared scallops with chive sauce on leek and carrot rice

Scallops are one of the most delicious shellfish. Organically farmed scallops feed on naturally occurring plankton and are a healthy food whose cultivation has a low environmental impact. Use fresh scallops, not frozen, as they exude less water during cooking.

SERVES 4

12–16 shelled scallops
45ml/3 tbsp olive oil
50g/2oz/¹⁄₃ cup wild rice
65g/2¹⁄₂oz/5 tbsp butter or 75ml/5 tbsp
   olive oil
4 carrots, cut into long thin strips
2 leeks, cut into thick, diagonal slices
1 small onion, finely chopped
115g/4oz/²⁄₃ cup long grain rice
1 fresh bay leaf

200ml/7fl oz/scant 1 cup white wine
450ml/³⁄₄ pint/scant 2 cups fish stock
60ml/4 tbsp double (heavy) cream or
   soya cream
a little lemon juice
25ml/1¹⁄₂ tbsp chopped fresh chives
30ml/2 tbsp chervil sprigs
sea salt and ground black pepper

1 Lightly season the shelled scallops, brush with 15ml/1 tbsp of the olive oil and set aside.

2 Cook the wild rice in a pan in plenty of boiling water for about 30 minutes or according to the packet instructions, until tender, then drain.

3 Heat half the butter or oil in a small frying pan and cook the carrot strips fairly gently for 4–5 minutes. Add the leek slices and fry for another 2 minutes. Season with sea salt and black pepper and add 30–45ml/2–3 tbsp water, then cover and cook the vegetables for a few minutes more. Uncover the pan and cook until the liquid has reduced. Set aside off the heat.

4 Melt half the remaining butter with 15ml/1 tbsp of the remaining oil in a heavy pan. Then add the onion and fry for 3–4 minutes, until softened but not browned.

5 Add the long grain rice and bay leaf to the pan and cook, stirring constantly, until the rice looks translucent and the grains are coated with oil.

6 Pour in half the wine and half the stock. Season with salt and bring to the boil. Stir, then cover and cook very gently for 15 minutes, or until the liquid is absorbed and the rice is tender.

7 Reheat the carrots and leeks gently, then stir them into the long grain rice with the wild rice. Taste and adjust the seasoning, if necessary. Meanwhile, pour the remaining wine and stock into a small pan and boil it rapidly until reduced by half.

8 Heat a heavy frying pan over a high heat. Add the remaining butter or oil. Add the scallops, and lightly sear them for 1–2 minutes on each side, then set aside and keep warm.

9 Pour the reduced stock and wine into the pan and heat until bubbling, then add the cream and boil until thickened. Season with lemon juice, sea salt and plenty of ground black pepper. Stir in the chopped chives and seared scallops.

10 Stir the chervil sprigs into the mixed rice and vegetables and pile it on to individual serving plates. Arrange the scallops on top and spoon the sauce over the rice. Serve immediately.

Nutritional information per portion: Energy 598kcal/2489kJ; Protein 30.8g; Carbohydrate 38.9g, of which sugars 6.3g; Fat 32g, of which saturates 15.3g; Cholesterol 108mg; Calcium 88mg; Fibre 3.1g; Sodium 321mg.

Salmon fish cakes

The secret of a good fish cake is to make it with freshly prepared fish and potatoes – organic of course – home-made breadcrumbs and plenty of fresh herbs, such as dill and parsley or tarragon. Serve simply with rocket leaves and lemon wedges.

SERVES 4

450g/1lb cooked salmon fillet
450g/1lb freshly cooked
    potatoes, mashed
25g/1oz/2 tbsp butter, melted or
    30ml/2 tbsp olive oil
10ml/2 tsp wholegrain mustard
15ml/1 tbsp each chopped fresh dill and
    chopped fresh parsley or tarragon
grated rind and juice of ½ lemon
15g/1½oz/2 tbsp wholemeal
    (whole-wheat) flour
1 egg, lightly beaten
150g/5oz/2 cups dried breadcrumbs
60ml/4 tbsp sunflower oil
sea salt and ground black pepper
rocket (arugula) leaves and chives,
    to garnish
lemon wedges, to serve

1 Flake the cooked salmon, discarding any skin and bones. Put it in a bowl with the mashed potato, melted butter or oil and wholegrain mustard, and mix well. Stir in the herbs and the lemon rind and juice. Season to taste with plenty of sea salt and ground black pepper.

2 Divide the mixture into eight portions and shape each into a ball, then flatten into a thick disc.

3 Dip the fish cakes first in flour, then in egg and finally in breadcrumbs, making sure that they are evenly coated with crumbs.

4 Heat the oil in a frying pan until it is very hot. Fry the fish cakes in batches until golden brown and crisp all over. As each batch is ready, drain on kitchen paper and keep hot. Garnish with rocket and chives and serve with lemon wedges.

Nutritional information per portion: Energy 586kcal/2453kJ; Protein 29.8g; Carbohydrate 49.9g, of which sugars 3.2g; Fat 31g, of which saturates 7.2g; Cholesterol 117mg; Calcium 79mg; Fibre 1.3g; Sodium 266mg.

Escalopes of chicken with vegetables

This quick, light dish is ideal as the weather warms up and easy meals become the order of the day. Flattening the chicken breasts thins and tenderizes the meat and speeds the cooking time.

SERVES 4

4 skinless, boneless chicken breast fillets, each weighing 175g/6oz
juice of 1 lime
120ml/4fl oz/½ cup olive oil
675g/1½lb mixed small new season potatoes, carrots, fennel (sliced if large), asparagus and peas
sea salt and ground black pepper
sprigs of fresh flat leaf parsley, to garnish

FOR THE TOMATO MAYONNAISE

150ml/¼ pint/⅔ cup mayonnaise
15ml/1 tbsp sun-dried tomato purée (paste)

1 Lay the chicken fillets between sheets of clear film (plastic wrap) or baking parchment and beat them evenly thin with a rolling pin. Season and sprinkle with lime juice.

2 Heat 45ml/3 tbsp of oil in a frying pan or griddle and cook the chicken escalopes for 10–12 minutes on each side, turning frequently.

3 In a small pan, season the new potatoes and carrots with sea salt, cover and cook with the remaining oil over a medium heat for 10–15 minutes, stirring frequently.

4 Add the fennel and cook for a further 5 minutes, stirring frequently. Finally, add the asparagus and peas and cook for 5 minutes more, or until all the vegetables are tender and cooked.

5 To make the tomato mayonnaise, mix together the mayonnaise and sun-dried tomato purée in a small bowl. Spoon the vegetables on to a warmed serving platter or individual plates and arrange the chicken on top. Serve the tomato mayonnaise with the chicken and vegetables. Garnish with sprigs of flat leaf parsley.

Nutritional information per portion: Energy 513kcal/2143kJ; Protein 44g; Carbohydrate 18.9g, of which sugars 9g; Fat 29.6g, of which saturates 4.7g; Cholesterol 141mg; Calcium 41mg; Fibre 3.2g; Sodium 251mg.

Chicken and asparagus risotto

Use fairly thick asparagus in this classic springtime risotto, as fine spears tend to overcook. The thick ends of the asparagus are full of flavour and they become beautifully tender in the time it takes for the rice to absorb the stock.

SERVES 4

75ml/5 tbsp olive oil
1 leek, finely chopped
115g/4oz/1¹/₂ cups oyster or brown cap
   (cremini) mushrooms, sliced
3 skinless, boneless chicken breast
   fillets, cubed

350g/12oz asparagus
250g/9oz/1¹/₄ cups risotto rice
900ml/1¹/₂ pints/3³/₄ cups simmering
   chicken stock
sea salt and ground black pepper
fresh Parmesan or premium Italian-style
   vegetarian cheese curls, to serve

1 Heat the olive oil in a pan. Add the finely chopped leek and cook gently until softened, but not coloured. Add the sliced mushrooms and cook for 5 minutes. Remove the vegetables from the pan and set aside.

2 Increase the heat and cook the cubes of chicken until golden on all sides. Do this in batches, if necessary, and then return them all to the pan.

3 Meanwhile, discard the woody ends from the asparagus and cut the spears in half. Set the tips aside. Cut the thick ends in half and add them to the pan. Return the leek and mushroom mixture to the pan and stir in the rice.

4 Pour in a ladleful of boiling stock and cook gently, stirring occasionally, until the stock is completely absorbed. Continue adding the stock a ladleful at a time, simmering until it is absorbed, the rice is tender and the chicken is cooked.

5 Add the asparagus tips with the last ladleful of boiling stock for the final 5 minutes and continue cooking the risotto very gently until the asparagus is tender. The whole process should take about 25–30 minutes.

6 Season the risotto to taste with salt and freshly ground black pepper and spoon it into individual warm serving bowls. Top each bowl with curls of cheese, and serve.

Nutritional information per portion: Energy 496kcal/2072kJ; Protein 36.1g; Carbohydrate 50g, of which sugars 2.7g; Fat 16.1g, of which saturates 7.4g; Cholesterol 105mg; Calcium 53mg; Fibre 2.7g; Sodium 148mg.

Roast leg of lamb

Tender young organic lamb is available only in the springtime, and is often served with a sauce using the first sprigs of mint of the year and early new potatoes.

SERVES 6

1.5kg/3¹/₄lb leg of lamb
4 garlic cloves, sliced
2 fresh rosemary sprigs
30ml/2 tbsp light olive oil
300ml/¹/₂ pint/1¹/₄ cups red wine
5ml/1 tsp honey
45ml/3 tbsp redcurrant jelly
sea salt and ground black pepper
spring vegetables, to serve

FOR THE ROAST POTATOES
45ml/3 tbsp olive oil
1.3kg/3lb potatoes, such as Desirée,
   peeled and cut into chunks

FOR THE MINT SAUCE
about 15g/¹/₂oz fresh mint
10ml/2 tsp unrefined caster (superfine)
   sugar or rapadura
15ml/1 tbsp boiling water
30ml/2 tbsp white wine vinegar

1 Heat the oven to 220°C/425°F/Gas 7. Make small slits all over the lamb. Press a slice of garlic and a few rosemary leaves into each, then place in a roasting pan and season well. Drizzle the oil over the lamb and roast for 1 hour.

2 Meanwhile, mix the wine, honey and redcurrant jelly in a small pan and heat, stirring, until the jelly melts. Bring to the boil, then reduce the heat and simmer until reduced by half. Spoon this glaze over the lamb and return it to the oven for 30–45 minutes.

3 Put the oil in a roasting pan on the shelf above the meat. Boil the potatoes for 5–10 minutes, then drain them and fluff up the surface with a fork. Add the potatoes to the hot oil and baste well. Roast for 45 minutes, or until crisp.

4 Place the mint on a chopping board and scatter sugar on top. Chop the mint finely, then transfer to a bowl. Add the boiling water and stir until the sugar has dissolved. Add 15ml/1 tbsp vinegar and taste the sauce before adding the remaining vinegar. (You may want to add slightly less or more than the suggested quantity.) Leave the mint sauce to stand until you are ready to serve the meal.

5 Remove the lamb from the oven, cover it loosely with foil and set it aside in a warm place to rest for 10–15 minutes before carving. Serve with the crisp roast potatoes, mint sauce and spring vegetables.

Nutritional information per portion: Energy 732kcal/3080kJ; Protein 78g; Carbohydrate 36.4g, of which sugars 4.2g; Fat 31.6g, of which saturates 12.7g; Cholesterol 257mg; Calcium 36mg; Fibre 2.2g; Sodium 182mg.

Lamb burgers with red onion and tomato relish

A sharp-sweet red onion relish works well with burgers based on Middle Eastern-style lamb. Try serving the burgers with pitta bread and tabbouleh for an authentic taste, though baked potatoes and a crisp green organic salad are also good accompaniments.

SERVES 4

25g/1oz/3 tbsp bulgur wheat
500g/1¼lb lean minced (ground) lamb
1 small red onion, finely chopped
2 garlic cloves, finely chopped
1 green chilli, seeded and finely chopped
5ml/1 tsp ground toasted cumin seeds
2.5ml/½ tsp ground sumac (optional)
15g/½oz/¼ cup chopped fresh flat
   leaf parsley
30ml/2 tbsp chopped fresh mint
olive oil, for frying
sea salt and ground black pepper

FOR THE RELISH
2 red (bell) peppers, halved and seeded
2 red onions, cut into 5mm/¼in thick slices

75–90ml/5–6 tbsp extra virgin olive oil
350g/12oz cherry tomatoes, chopped
½–1 fresh red or green chilli, seeded and
   finely chopped (optional)
30ml/2 tbsp chopped fresh mint
30ml/2 tbsp chopped fresh parsley
15ml/1 tbsp chopped fresh oregano
   or marjoram
2.5–5ml/½–1 tsp each ground toasted
   cumin seeds
2.5–5ml/½–1 tsp sumac (optional)
juice of ½ lemon
unrefined caster (superfine) sugar or
   rapadura, to taste

1 Pour 150ml/¼ pint/⅔ cup hot water over the bulgur wheat in a mixing bowl and leave to stand for 15 minutes, then drain the wheat in a sieve (strainer) and squeeze out the excess moisture.

2 To make the relish, grill (broil) the peppers, skin side up, until the skin chars and blisters. Place in a bowl, cover and leave to stand for 10 minutes. Peel off the skin, dice the peppers finely and place in a bowl.

3 Brush the onions with 15ml/1 tbsp oil and grill for 5 minutes on each side, until browned. Leave to cool.

4 Place the bulgur in a bowl and add the minced lamb, onion, garlic, chilli, cumin, sumac, if using, parsley and mint. Mix the ingredients thoroughly together by hand, then season with 2.5ml/½ tsp salt and plenty of black pepper and mix again. Form the mixture into eight small burgers.

5 Chop the onions for the relish. Add with the tomatoes, chilli to taste, herbs and 2.5ml/^{1}/$_2$ tsp each of the cumin and sumac, if using, to the peppers. Stir in 60ml/4 tbsp of the remaining oil and 15ml/1 tbsp of the lemon juice. Season with salt, pepper and sugar and leave to stand for 20–30 minutes.

6 Heat a heavy frying pan over a high heat and grease lightly with olive oil. Cook the burgers for about 5–6 minutes on each side, or until just cooked at the centre.

7 While the burgers are cooking, taste the relish and adjust the seasoning, adding more pepper, sugar, oil, chilli, cumin, sumac, if using, and lemon juice to taste. Serve the burgers with the relish.

Nutritional information per portion: Energy 537kcal/2228kJ; Protein 27.2g; Carbohydrate 19g, of which sugars 13.4g; Fat 39.6g, of which saturates 11.1g; Cholesterol 96mg; Calcium 83mg; Fibre 4.2g; Sodium 105mg.

Lamb stew with new potatoes and shallots

This fresh lemon-seasoned stew is finished with an Italian mixture of chopped garlic, parsley and lemon rind known as gremolata, the traditional topping for osso bucco.

SERVES 6

1kg/2¹/₄lb boneless shoulder of lamb,
   trimmed of fat and cut into 5cm/2in cubes
1 garlic clove, finely chopped
finely grated rind of ¹/₂ lemon; juice of 1 lemon
90ml/6 tbsp olive oil
45ml/3 tbsp wholemeal (whole-wheat) flour
1 large onion, sliced
5 anchovy fillets in olive oil, drained
2.5ml/¹/₂ tsp unrefined caster (superfine)
   sugar or rapadura
300ml/¹/₂ pint/1¹/₄ cups fruity white wine
475ml/16fl oz/2 cups lamb stock or half
   stock and half water

1 fresh bay leaf
fresh rosemary sprig
fresh parsley sprig
500g/1¹/₄lb small new potatoes
250g/9oz shallots, peeled but left whole
45ml/3 tbsp double (heavy) cream or
   soya cream (optional)
sea salt and ground black pepper

FOR THE GREMOLATA
1 garlic clove, finely chopped
finely shredded rind of ¹/₂ lemon
45ml/3 tbsp chopped fresh flat leaf parsley

1 Mix the lamb, garlic and the rind and juice of ¹/₂ lemon in a non-metallic container. Season with pepper, mix in 15ml/1 tbsp olive oil and marinate in the refrigerator for 12–24 hours. Drain the lamb, reserving the marinade, and pat dry with kitchen paper. Heat the oven to 180°C/350°F/Gas 4.

2 Heat 30ml/2 tbsp olive oil in a large, heavy frying pan. Toss the lamb in flour seasoned with salt and pepper, shaking off any excess flour. Add to the pan, in small batches. Seal on all sides in the hot oil, stirring constantly with a wooden spoon.

3 As each batch browns, transfer it to a flame-proof casserole. If necessary, add an extra 15ml/1 tbsp olive oil to the pan.

4 Reduce the heat, add 15ml/1 tbsp oil to the pan and gently cook the sliced onion, stirring frequently, for 10 minutes until soft and golden but not browned. Add the anchovy fillets and sugar, and cook, mashing the anchovies into the onion with a wooden spoon.

5 Add the reserved marinade, increase the heat a little and cook for 1–2 minutes, then pour in the fruity white wine and lamb stock, or lamb stock and water, and bring to the boil. Simmer the sauce gently for about 5 minutes, then pour the sauce over the lamb in the pan or casserole.

6 Tie the bay leaf, rosemary and parsley together to make a bouquet garni and add to the lamb. Season the stew, then cover tightly and cook in the oven for 1 hour. Add the potatoes to the stew and stir well, then return the stew to the oven and cook for a further 20 minutes.

7 To make the gremolata, chop the garlic, lemon rind and parsley together finely. Cover and set aside in a dish.

8 Heat the remaining olive oil in a frying pan and brown the shallots on all sides, then stir them into the lamb stew. Cover and cook the stew for a further 30–40 minutes until the lamb is tender. Transfer the lamb and vegetables to a warmed serving dish and keep hot. Discard the bunch of herbs.

9 Boil the remaining cooking juices to reduce, then add the double cream or soya cream, if using, and simmer for 2–3 minutes. Adjust the seasoning, adding a little lemon juice to taste if liked. Pour this sauce over the lamb, scatter the gremolata mixture over the top and serve immediately.

Nutritional information per portion: Energy 553kcal/2311kJ; Protein 37g; Carbohydrate 26.2g, of which sugars 5.3g; Fat 30.6g, of which saturates 10.4g; Cholesterol 128mg; Calcium 79mg; Fibre 2.7g; Sodium 261mg.

Frozen clementines

These pretty, sorbet-filled fruits store well in the freezer, so make them well in advance and they will be perfect for an impromptu dinner party.

MAKES 12

16 large clementines or small oranges
175g/6oz/scant 1 cup unrefined caster
   (superfine) sugar or rapadura
105ml/7 tbsp water
juice of 2 lemons
a little fresh orange juice (if necessary)
fresh mint leaves, to decorate

1 Slice the tops off 12 of the clementines to make lids. Set aside on a baking sheet. Scoop the flesh into a bowl, keeping the shells intact. Add the shells to the lids, then freeze.

2 Gently heat and stir the sugar and water in a heavy pan until the sugar dissolves. Boil for 3 minutes without stirring, then leave to cool. Stir in the lemon juice.

3 Finely grate the rind from the remaining clementines. Squeeze the fruits and add the juice and rind to the syrup.

4 Process the clementine flesh in a food processor or blender, strain over a bowl and add to the syrup. You need about 900ml/1¹⁄₂ pints/3³⁄₄ cups of liquid. Top up with fresh orange juice if necessary.

5 Pour into a shallow container and freeze for 3–4 hours, beating twice. Pack the sorbet into the clementine shells, position the lids and freeze overnight.

6 Transfer the clementines to the refrigerator 30 minutes before serving on individual plates.

Nutritional information per portion: Energy 117kcal/499kJ; Protein 1.8g; Carbohydrate 28.9g, of which sugars 28.9g; Fat 0.2g, of which saturates 0g; Cholesterol 0mg; Calcium 83mg; Fibre 2.7g; Sodium 9mg.

Rhubarb and ginger ice cream

The tangy combination of gently poached rhubarb and chopped ginger is blended with mascarpone to create this pretty blush-pink ice cream.

SERVES 4–6

5 pieces of preserved stem ginger
450g/1lb trimmed rhubarb, sliced
115g/4oz/generous ¹/₂ cup unrefined
    caster (superfine) sugar or rapadura
30ml/2 tbsp water
150g/5oz/²/₃ cup mascarpone
150ml/¹/₄ pint/²/₃ cup whipping cream
    or soya cream
wafer baskets, to serve (optional)

1 Using a sharp knife, roughly chop the stem ginger and set it aside. Put the rhubarb slices into a pan and add the sugar and water. Cover and simmer for 5 minutes until the rhubarb is just tender and still bright pink.

2 Tip the mixture into a food processor or blender, process until smooth, then leave to cool. Chill, if time permits.

3 Mix together the mascarpone, cream and ginger with the rhubarb purée; or churn them with the rhubarb purée in an ice cream maker for 15–20 minutes until thick.

4 Pour the mixture into a plastic tub or other freezerproof container and freeze for 6 hours or until firm, beating once or twice with a fork or an electric whisk to break up the ice crystals

Nutritional information per portion: Energy 221kcal/924kJ; Protein 3.6g; Carbohydrate 22.1g, of which sugars 22.1g; Fat 13.8g, of which saturates 8.6g; Cholesterol 37mg; Calcium 94mg; Fibre 1.1g; Sodium 10mg.

Banana and apricot caramel trifle

Organic bananas are an excellent source of potassium and good for the digestion – making this an irresistible dessert for a special occasion. Ginger cake adds sharpness to the creamy flavours.

SERVES 6–8

300ml/1/2 pint/11/4 cups milk or soya milk

1 vanilla pod (bean), or 4–5 drops
vanilla extract

45ml/3 tbsp unrefined caster (superfine)
sugar or rapadura

20ml/4 tsp cornflour (cornstarch)

3 egg yolks

60ml/4 tbsp apricot conserve (jam)

175–225g/6–8oz ginger cake, cubed

3 bananas, sliced, with one reserved
for topping

115g/4oz/generous 1/2 cup granulated
(white) sugar or rapadura

300ml/1/2 pint/11/4 cups double (heavy)
cream or soya cream

a few drops of lemon juice

1 Pour the milk into a small pan. Carefully split the vanilla pod (if using) down the middle and scrape the tiny seeds into the pan.

2 Add the vanilla pod, or extract, to the milk and bring to the boil. Remove from the heat and set aside. When the milk has cooled slightly, remove the pod.

3 Whisk together the sugar, cornflour and eggs until pale and creamy. Whisk in the milk and return to the pan. Heat to simmering point, stirring all the time. Cook gently until the custard coats the back of a wooden spoon thickly.

4 Leave to cool, covered tightly with clear film (plastic wrap). Ensure the clear film is pressed against the surface of the custard to prevent a skin forming.

5 In a pan, gently heat the apricot conserve and 60ml/4 tbsp water for 2–3 minutes, stirring. Put the cubed cake in a deep serving bowl or dish and pour on the apricot preserve. Cover with sliced bananas, then the custard. Chill for 1–2 hours.

6 Dissolve the sugar in a small pan with 60ml/4 tbsp water and then cook until it is just turning golden. Immediately pour on to a sheet of foil and leave to harden, then break into pieces.

7 Whip the cream into soft peaks and spread it evenly over the custard. Chill the trifle for 2–3 hours, then top with sliced banana, dipped into lemon juice, and the cracked caramel pieces.

Nutritional information per portion: Energy 452kcal/1893kJ; Protein 4.8g; Carbohydrate 53.8g, of which sugars 44.1g; Fat 25.7g, of which saturates 13.6g; Cholesterol 129mg; Calcium 104mg; Fibre 0.7g; Sodium 77mg.

Ricotta cheesecake

This Sicilian-style cheesecake makes good use of ricotta's firm texture. The cheese is enriched with eggs and cream and enlivened with the unwaxed grated rind of organic orange and lemon.

SERVES 8

450g/1lb/2 cups ricotta cheese
120ml/4fl oz/¹/₂ cup double (heavy)
    cream or soya cream
2 eggs
1 egg yolk
75g/3oz/6 tbsp unrefined caster
    (superfine) sugar or rapadura
finely grated rind of 1 orange and
    1 lemon, plus extra to decorate

FOR THE PASTRY

175g/6oz/1¹/₂ cups plain
    (all-purpose) flour
45ml/3 tbsp unrefined caster (superfine)
    sugar or rapadura
115g/4oz/¹/₂ cup chilled butter, diced
1 egg yolk

1 Sift the flour and sugar on to a cold surface. Make a well in the centre for the butter and egg yolk. Work the flour into the butter and egg yolk.

2 Gather the dough together, reserve a quarter and press the rest into a 23cm/9in fluted flan tin (pan) with a removable base, and chill.

3 Preheat the oven to 190°C/375°F/ Gas 5. In a bowl, beat well the cheese, cream, eggs, yolk, sugar and rinds.

4 Prick the bottom of the pastry case, then line with foil and fill with baking beans. Bake for 15 minutes.

5 Transfer to a wire rack, remove the foil and beans and allow the pastry to cool in the tin.

6 Spoon the cheese and cream filling into the pastry case, and level. Roll out the reserved dough, cut into long, even strips and arrange them on top of the filling in a lattice pattern. Stick them in place with water.

7 Bake for 30–35 minutes until golden and set. Leave to cool on a wire rack, then carefully remove the side of the tin. Transfer to a serving plate with a metal spatula. Decorate before serving.

Nutritional information per portion: Energy 449kcal/1873kJ; Protein 9.9g; Carbohydrate 34.8g, of which sugars 18.1g; Fat 31.1g, of which saturates 18.4g; Cholesterol 173mg; Calcium 62mg; Fibre 0.7g; Sodium 112mg.

Citrus and caramel custards

Wonderfully smooth, these custards are delicately scented with tangy citrus flavours and aromatic cinamon. Use organic milk for a healthier, tastier dish.

SERVES 4

450ml/³/₄ pint/scant 2 cups milk or
  soya milk
150ml/¹/₄ pint/²/₃ cup single (light)
  cream or soya cream
1 cinnamon stick, broken in half
thinly pared rind of ¹/₂ lemon
thinly pared rind of ¹/₂ orange
4 egg yolks
5ml/1 tsp cornflour (cornstarch)
40g/1¹/₂oz/3 tbsp unrefined caster
  (superfine) sugar or rapadura
grated rind of ¹/₂ lemon
grated rind of ¹/₂ orange
unrefined icing (confectioners') sugar,
  to dust

1 Place the milk and cream in a pan. Add the cinnamon stick halves and the strips of pared lemon and orange rind. Bring to the boil, then reduce the heat and simmer for 10 minutes.

2 Preheat the oven to 160°C/325°F/ Gas 3. Whisk the egg yolks, cornflour and sugar together. Remove the rinds and cinnamon from the hot milk and cream and discard. Whisk the hot milk and cream into the egg yolk mixture.

3 Add the grated citrus rind to the custard mixture and stir through. Pour into four dishes (13cm/5in in diameter). Place in a roasting pan and pour in warm water three-quarters of the way up. Bake for 25 minutes, or until the custards are just set. Remove the dishes from the water; leave to cool, then chill.

4 Preheat the grill (broiler) to high. Sprinkle the custards with icing sugar and grill until the tops turn golden brown and caramelize.

Nutritional information per portion: Energy 229kcal/958kJ; Protein 8g; Carbohydrate 17.7g, of which sugars 16.6g; Fat 14.6g, of which saturates 7.3g; Cholesterol 229mg; Calcium 197mg; Fibre 0g; Sodium 70mg.

Rhubarb meringue pie

The sharp tang of tender forced rhubarb with its sweet meringue topping will really tantalize the taste buds. This pudding is delicious hot or cold with cream or vanilla ice cream. Rhubarb, whether early forced or maincrop, should be cooked with sugar and a tablespoon or two of water.

SERVES 6

200g/7oz/1¾ cups plain (all-purpose) flour, plus extra for flouring
25g/1oz/¼ cup ground walnuts
115g/4oz/½ cup chilled butter or non-hydrogenated magarine, diced
275g/10oz/generous 1½ cups unrefined caster (superfine) sugar or rapadura

4 egg yolks
675g/1½lb rhubarb, cut into small pieces
grated rind and juice of 3 oranges
75ml/5 tbsp cornflour (cornstarch)
3 egg whites
whipped cream or soya cream, to serve

1 Sift the flour into a bowl and add the ground walnuts. Rub in the butter until the mixture resembles fine breadcrumbs.

2 Stir in 30ml/2 tbsp of sugar and 1 egg yolk beaten with 15ml/1 tbsp water. Mix to a firm dough. Turn out on to a floured surface and knead. Wrap in a plastic bag and chill for 30 minutes.

3 Preheat the oven to 190°C/375°F/Gas 5. Roll out the pastry on a floured surface and use to line a 23cm/9in fluted flan tin (pan). Prick the base with a fork. Line with cooking foil and fill with baking beans. Then bake for 15 minutes.

4 Put the rhubarb, 75g/3oz/6 tbsp of the remaining sugar and the orange rind in a pan. Cover and cook gently until the rhubarb is tender.

5 Remove the foil and beans from the pastry case, then brush with a little of the remaining egg yolk. Bake for 10–15 minutes until the pastry is crisp.

6 Blend together the cornflour and the orange juice in a small bowl. Remove the rhubarb from the heat, stir the cornflour mixture into it, then bring back to the boil, stirring until thickened. Cook for 1–2 minutes. Leave to cool slightly, then beat in the remaining egg yolks. Pour into the cooked pastry case, spreading it evenly.

7 In a large mixing bowl, whisk the egg whites into soft peaks, then gradually whisk in the remaining sugar, 15ml/1 tbsp at a time, whisking well each time.

8 Spoon the meringue over the filling to cover completely. Bake for 25 minutes until golden. Serve warm, or leave to cool for 30 minutes. Serve with whipped cream.

Nutritional information per portion: Energy 567kcal/2388kJ; Protein 8.4g; Carbohydrate 89.5g, of which sugars 52.6g; Fat 22g, of which saturates 11.1g; Cholesterol 136mg; Calcium 202mg; Fibre 2.8g; Sodium 168mg.

Russian poppy seed cake

This plain, simple cake, flavoured with lemon and vanilla, and studded with tiny black organic poppy seeds, has a distinctive, utterly delicious taste.

SERVES ABOUT 8

130g/4¹/₂oz/generous 1 cup self-raising (self-rising) flour
5ml/1 tsp baking powder
2 eggs
225g/8oz/generous 1 cup unrefined caster (superfine) sugar or rapadura
5–10ml/1–2 tsp vanilla extract
200g/7oz/scant 1¹/₂ cups poppy seeds, ground
15ml/1 tbsp grated lemon rind
120ml/4fl oz/¹/₂ cup milk or soya milk
130g/4¹/₂oz/generous ¹/₂ cup unsalted (sweet) butter or non-hydrogenated margarine, melted and cooled
30ml/2 tbsp sunflower oil
unrefined icing (confectioners') sugar, sifted, for dusting
whipped cream or soya cream, to serve

1 Preheat the oven to 180°C/350°F/Gas 4. Grease a deep 23cm/9in round springform cake tin (pan). Sift together the flour and baking powder.

2 Using an electric whisk, beat together the eggs, sugar and vanilla extract for 4–5 minutes until pale and fluffy. Then stir in the poppy seeds and the lemon rind.

3 Gently fold the sifted ingredients into the egg and poppy seed mixture, in three batches, alternating with the milk, then fold in the melted butter or margarine and sunflower oil.

4 Pour the mixture into the tin and bake for 40 minutes, or until firm. Cool in the tin for 15 minutes, then invert on to a wire rack. Leave until cold, dust with icing sugar and serve with cream.

Nutritional information per portion: Energy 485kcal/2023kJ; Protein 8.3g; Carbohydrate 42.7g, of which sugars 30.5g; Fat 32.4g, of which saturates 11.4g; Cholesterol 83mg; Calcium 267mg; Fibre 2.5g; Sodium 188mg.

Double-ginger cake

Preserved stem ginger and organic root ginger, which is smaller and has a more intense flavour than the non-organic variety, are used in this tasty tea bread.

SERVES 8–10

3 eggs

225g/8oz/generous 1 cup unrefined
caster (superfine) sugar or rapadura

250ml/8fl oz/1 cup sunflower oil

5ml/1 tsp vanilla extract

15ml/1 tbsp syrup from a jar of
preserved stem ginger

225g/8oz courgettes (zucchini), grated

2.5cm/1in piece fresh root ginger, peeled
and finely grated

350g/12oz/3 cups unbleached plain
(all-purpose) flour

5ml/1 tsp baking powder

5ml/1 tsp ground cinnamon

2 pieces preserved stem ginger, drained
and finely chopped

15ml/1 tbsp unrefined demerara (raw)
sugar or rapadura

butter, to serve (optional)

1 Preheat the oven to 190°C/375°F/Gas 5. Beat together the eggs and sugar until light and fluffy. Slowly beat in the oil until the mixture forms a batter. Mix in the vanilla extract and ginger syrup, then stir in the grated courgettes and fresh ginger.

2 Sift together the flour and baking powder in a large bowl. Add the cinnamon and mix well. Stir the dried ingredients into the courgette mixture.

3 Lightly grease a 900g/2lb loaf tin (pan) and pour in the courgette mixture, making sure it fills the corners. Smooth and level the top.

4 Mix together the chopped stem ginger and demerara sugar in a small bowl, then sprinkle the mixture evenly over the surface of the courgette mixture.

5 Bake for 1 hour, or until a skewer comes out clean when inserted into the centre. Leave to cool in the tin (pan) for 20 minutes, then turn out on to a wire rack and leave to cool completely. Serve in slices with butter, if you like.

Nutritional information per portion: Energy 403kcal/1691kJ; Protein 5.7g; Carbohydrate 54.3g, of which sugars 27.6g; Fat 19.7g, of which saturates 2.7g; Cholesterol 57mg; Calcium 77mg; Fibre 1.3g; Sodium 24mg.

Summer

This season is a gift for any cook. Chilled

dishes are easy to prepare in advance, while

salads allow you to make the most of the

plentiful supply of fruit and vegetables.

It's also the perfect time to cook, and

entertain, outside. And, with a wide selection

of mouthwatering fruits in season, summer

desserts really are something special.

Vichyssoise

This classic, chilled summer soup is based on the flavourful combination of leeks and potatoes, made luxuriously velvety by adding dairy or soya cream.

SERVES 4–6

50g/2oz/¹/₄ cup unsalted (sweet) butter
  or 50ml/3¹/₂ tbsp olive oil
450g/1lb leeks, white parts only, sliced
3 large shallots, sliced
250g/9oz floury potatoes (such as Maris
  Piper), peeled and cut into chunks
1 litre/1³/₄ pints/4 cups light chicken
  stock or water
300ml/¹/₂ pint/1¹/₄ cups double (heavy)
  cream or soya cream
a little lemon juice (optional)
sea salt and ground black pepper
fresh chives, to garnish

1 Heat the butter or oil in a heavy pan. Add the leeks and shallots, cover and cook gently for 15–20 minutes until soft but not browned.

2 Add the potato chunks to the pan and cook, uncovered, for a few minutes, stirring occasionally.

3 Stir in the chicken stock or water, 5ml/1 tsp sea salt and ground pepper to taste. Bring to the boil, reduce the heat and partly cover the pan. Simmer until the potatoes are soft.

4 Allow to cool and then process the soup until smooth in a food processor or blender. Pour the soup into a bowl and stir in the cream. Season to taste.

5 Chill the soup for at least 4 hours or until it is very cold. Taste the chilled soup to see if it requires seasoning and add to taste. You can also add a squeeze of lemon juice, if required. Then pour the soup into bowls and garnish with chives.

Nutritional information per portion: Energy 362kcal/1494kJ; Protein 3g; Carbohydrate 11.1g, of which sugars 4g; Fat 34.2g, of which saturates 21.2g; Cholesterol 86mg; Calcium 51mg; Fibre 2.3g; Sodium 68mg.

Tabbouleh

This is a wonderfully refreshing, tangy salad of soaked bulgur wheat and masses of fresh organic mint and parsley. Increase the amount of fresh herbs for a greener salad.

SERVES 4–6

250g/9oz/1½ cups bulgur wheat
1 large bunch spring onions (scallions),
    thinly sliced
1 cucumber, finely chopped or diced
3 tomatoes, chopped
1.5–2.5ml/¼–½ tsp ground cumin
1 large bunch fresh flat leaf
    parsley, chopped
1 large bunch fresh mint, chopped
juice of 2 lemons, or to taste
60ml/4 tbsp extra virgin olive oil
cos or romaine lettuce leaves
olives, lemon wedges, tomato wedges,
    cucumber slices and mint sprigs, to
    garnish (optional)
natural (plain) yogurt, to serve (optional)

1 Remove any dirt from the bulgur wheat. Place it in a bowl, cover with cold water and leave to soak for about 30 minutes. Tip the bulgur wheat into a sieve (strainer) and drain well, shaking to remove any excess water, then return it to the bowl.

2 Add the spring onions to the bulgur wheat, then mix and squeeze together with your hands to combine.

3 Add the cucumber, tomatoes, cumin, parsley, mint, lemon juice and oil to the bulgur wheat and toss well.

4 Heap the tabbouleh on to a bed of lettuce leaves and garnish with olives, lemon wedges, tomato, cucumber and mint sprigs. Serve with a bowl of natural yogurt, if you like.

Nutritional information per portion: Energy 232kcal/965kJ; Protein 5.2g; Carbohydrate 34.6g, of which sugars 2.7g; Fat 8.4g, of which saturates 1.1g; Cholesterol 0mg; Calcium 51mg; Fibre 1.4g; Sodium 12mg.

Cold somen noodles

At the height of summer, cold somen noodles served immersed in ice cold water and accompanied by sauces and relishes make a refreshing and exotic meal.

SERVES 4

300g/11oz dried somen or soba noodles

FOR THE DIPPING SAUCE
105ml/7 tbsp mirin
2.5ml/½ tsp sea salt
105ml/7 tbsp shoyu
20g/¾oz kezuri-bushi
400ml/14fl oz/1⅔ cups water

FOR THE RELISHES
2 spring onions (scallions), trimmed and
    finely chopped
2.5cm/1in fresh root ginger, peeled and
    finely grated

2 shiso or basil leaves, finely
    chopped (optional)
30ml/2 tbsp toasted sesame seeds

FOR THE GARNISHES
10cm/4in cucumber
5ml/1 tsp sea salt
ice cubes or a block of ice
ice-cold water
115g/4oz cooked, peeled small
    prawns (shrimp)
orchid flowers or nasturtium flowers
    and leaves (optional)

1 To make the dipping sauce, put the mirin in a pan and bring to the boil to evaporate the alcohol. Add the salt and shoyu and shake the pan gently to mix. Add the kezuri-bushi and mix with the liquid. Add the water to the pan and bring to the boil. Cook over a vigorous heat for 3 minutes without stirring. Remove from the heat and strain through a muslin (cheesecloth) bag. Leave to cool, then chill for at least an hour.

2 Prepare the cucumber garnish. If the cucumber is bigger than 4cm/1½in in diameter, cut in half and scoop out the seeds, then slice thinly. For a smaller cucumber, first cut into 5cm/2in lengths, then use a vegetable peeler to remove the seeds and make a hole in the centre. Slice thinly. Sprinkle with the salt and leave in a sieve (strainer) for 20 minutes, then rinse in cold water and drain.

3 Bring at least 1.5 litres/2½ pints/6¼ cups water to the boil in a large pan. Meanwhile, untie the bundle of somen. Have 75ml/2½fl oz/⅓ cup cold water to hand. Somen only take 2 minutes to cook. Put the somen in the rapidly boiling water. When it foams again, pour the glass of water in. When the water boils again, the somen are ready. Drain into a colander. Rinse under cold running water, and rub the somen with your hands to remove the starch. Drain well.

4 Put some ice cubes or a block of ice in the centre of a chilled, large glass bowl, and add the somen. Gently pour on enough ice-cold water to cover the somen, then arrange cucumber slices, prawns and flowers, if using, on top.

5 Prepare all the relishes separately in small dishes or small sake cups.

6 Divide approximately one-third of the dipping sauce among four small cups. Put the remaining sauce in a jug (pitcher) or gravy boat.

7 Serve the noodles cold with the relishes. The guests are invited to put any combination of relishes into their dipping-sauce cup. Hold the cup over the somen bowl, pick up a mouthful of somen, then dip them into the sauce and eat. Add more dipping sauce from the jug and more relishes as required.

Nutritional information per portion: Energy 445kcal/1885kJ; Protein 16.3g; Carbohydrate 79.2g, of which sugars 23.7g; Fat 9.2g, of which saturates 0.7g; Cholesterol 56mg; Calcium 109mg; Fibre 2.9g; Sodium 2420mg.

Garlic mayonnaise

Fresh wet organic garlic is available in spring and summer, but try to use dried, cured bulbs for this mouthwatering creamy mayonnaise as they have a more pungent flavour.

SERVES 4–6

2 large egg yolks
pinch of dried mustard
about 300ml/¹/₂ pint/1¹/₄ cups mild
   olive oil
15–30ml/1–2 tbsp lemon juice, white
   wine vinegar or warm water
2–4 garlic cloves
sea salt and ground black pepper

1 When the egg yolks and oil are at room temperature, mix the yolks, mustard and a pinch of salt in a bowl.

2 Whisk in the oil, one drop at a time. When almost half has been fully used, start to add it in a slow, steady stream, whisking all the time.

3 As the mayonnaise starts to thicken, thin it with a few drops of lemon juice, vinegar or a few teaspoons of warm water.

4 When the mayonnaise is as thick as soft butter, stop adding oil. Season the mayonnaise to taste and add more lemon juice or vinegar as required.

5 Crush the garlic with the blade of a knife and stir it into the mayonnaise. For a slightly milder flavour, blanch the garlic twice in plenty of boiling water, then purée the cloves before beating them into the mayonnaise.

Nutritional information per portion:Energy 323kcal/1330kJ; Protein 1.2g; Carbohydrate 0.6g, of which sugars 0.1g; Fat 35.2g, of which saturates 5.3g; Cholesterol 67mg; Calcium 9mg; Fibre 0.1g; Sodium 3mg.

Guacamole

There are many different types of organic onion now available; this chunky guacamole uses sweet red onion for flavour and colour. Serve as a dip or sauce.

SERVES 4

2 large ripe avocados
1 small red onion, very finely chopped
1 red or green chilli, seeded and very
    finely chopped
1/2–1 garlic clove, crushed with a little
    sea salt
finely shredded rind of 1/2 lime and juice
    of 1–1 1/2 limes
225g/8oz tomatoes, seeded and chopped
30ml/2 tbsp roughly chopped fresh
    coriander (cilantro)
2.5–5ml/1/2–1 tsp ground toasted
    cumin seeds
15ml/1 tbsp olive oil
15–30ml/1–2 tbsp sour cream (optional)
sea salt and ground black pepper
lime wedges dipped in sea salt (optional),
    and fresh coriander sprigs, to garnish

1 Cut one of the avocados in half and lift out and discard the stone (pit). Scrape the flesh from both halves into a bowl and mash it roughly with a fork.

2 Add the onion, chilli, garlic, lime rind, tomatoes and coriander and stir well to mix. Add the ground cumin and seasoning to taste, then stir in the olive oil.

3 Halve and stone (pit) the remaining avocado. Dice the flesh and stir it into the guacamole.

4 Squeeze in fresh lime juice to taste, mix well, cover and leave for 15 minutes so that the flavour develops. Stir in the sour cream, if using. Serve with lime wedges dipped in sea salt, if you wish, and garnish with fresh coriander sprigs

Nutritional information per portion. Energy 108kcal/446kJ; Protein 1.6g; Carbohydrate 3.2g, of which sugars 2.3g; Fat 9.9g, of which saturates 2.1g; Cholesterol 0mg; Calcium 13mg; Fibre 2.3g; Sodium 8mg.

Summer salad

Ripe organic tomatoes, mozzarella and olives make a good base for a fresh and tangy pasta salad that is perfect for a light summer lunch.

SERVES 4

350g/12oz/3 cups dried penne

150g/5oz packet buffalo mozzarella,
     drained and diced

3 ripe tomatoes, diced

10 pitted black olives, sliced

10 pitted green olives, sliced

1 spring onion (scallion), thinly sliced on the diagonal

1 handful fresh basil leaves

FOR THE DRESSING

90ml/6 tbsp extra virgin olive oil

15ml/1 tbsp balsamic vinegar or lemon juice

sea salt and ground black pepper

1 Cook the pasta for 10–12 minutes, or according to the instructions on the packet. Tip it into a colander and rinse briefly under cold running water, then shake the colander to remove as much water as possible and leave to drain.

2 Make the dressing. Whisk the olive oil and balsamic vinegar or lemon juice in a jug (pitcher) with a little salt and pepper to taste.

3 Place the pasta, mozzarella, tomatoes, olives and spring onion in a large bowl, pour the dressing over and toss together well. Taste for seasoning before serving, sprinkled with basil leaves.

Nutritional information per portion: Energy 635kcal/2658kJ; Protein 18.7g; Carbohydrate 67.3g, of which sugars 5.3g; Fat 34.2g, of which saturates 9.1g; Cholesterol 22mg; Calcium 210mg; Fibre 5.5g; Sodium 1845mg.

Country pasta salad

Colourful, tasty and nutritious, this is the ideal pasta salad for a summer picnic. Any medium-sized pasta shapes are suitable for this salad.

SERVES 6

300g/11oz/2³/₄ cups dried fusilli

150g/5oz French (green) beans, trimmed and cut
     into 5cm/2in lengths

1 potato, about 150g/5oz, diced

200g/7oz cherry tomatoes, halved

2 spring onions (scallions), finely chopped

90g/3¹/₂oz/scant 1¹/₄ cups Parmesan cheese or premium
     Italian-style vegetarian cheese, coarsely shaved

6–8 pitted black olives, cut into rings

15–30ml/1–2 tbsp capers, to taste

FOR THE DRESSING

90ml/6 tbsp extra virgin olive oil

15ml/1 tbsp balsamic vinegar

15ml/1 tbsp chopped fresh flat leaf parsley

sea salt and ground black pepper

1 Cook the pasta according to the instructions on the packet. Drain it into a colander, rinse with cold water until cold, shake and leave to drain and dry.

2 Boil the beans and diced potato for 5–6 minutes or steam for 8–10 minutes. Drain and let cool.

3 To make the dressing, whisk all the ingredients in a large bowl with a little sea salt and ground black pepper. Add the tomatoes, spring onions, Parmesan, olive rings and capers to the dressing, then stir in the cold pasta, beans and potato. Toss well to mix. Cover and leave to stand for 30 minutes. Taste for seasoning before serving.

Nutritional information per portion: Energy 381kcal/1600kJ; Protein 13.3g; Carbohydrate 44.4g, of which sugars 3.8g; Fat 18g, of which saturates 5g; Cholesterol 15mg; Calcium 212mg; Fibre 2.9g; Sodium 341mg.

Provençal aïoli with smoked haddock

This substantial salad is a meal on its own and perfect for summer entertaining. Choose organic vegetables and vary them according to what is in season as the summer progresses.

SERVES 6

1kg/2¼lb smoked haddock
bouquet garni
18 small new potatoes, scrubbed
1 large or 2 small fresh mint sprigs, torn
225g/8oz French (green) beans, trimmed
225g/8oz broccoli florets
6 eggs, hard-boiled
12 baby carrots, with leaves if
    possible, scrubbed
1 large red (bell) pepper, seeded and cut
    into strips
2 fennel bulbs, cut into strips

18 red or yellow cherry tomatoes
sea salt
6 large whole cooked prawns (shrimp)
    or langoustines, in the shell, to
    garnish (optional)

FOR THE AIOLI

600ml/1 pint/2½ cups home-made or
    good-quality bought mayonnaise
2 fat garlic cloves (or more if you
    prefer), crushed
cayenne pepper

1 Put the smoked haddock into a sauté pan with enough water barely to cover the fish. Add the bouquet garni. Bring to the boil, cover and poach gently for 10 minutes until the fish flakes easily. Drain, discard the bouquet garni and set aside.

2 Cook the potatoes with the mint in a pan of lightly salted boiling water until just tender. Drain and set aside.

3 Cook the beans and broccoli in separate pans of lightly salted boiling water for 5 minutes. Refresh the vegetables under cold water, drain again, then set aside.

4 Remove the skin from the fish and break it into large flakes. Shell the eggs and halve lengthways. Pile the haddock in the middle of a large serving platter. Arrange the eggs and all the vegetables round the edges or randomly. Garnish with the prawns or langoustines if you are using them.

5 To make the aïoli, put the mayonnaise in a bowl. Stir in the crushed garlic and cayenne pepper to taste. Serve in individual bowls or one large bowl to hand round.

Nutritional information per portion: Energy 1099kcal/4567kJ; Protein 66.5g; Carbohydrate 21.4g, of which sugars 10.2g; Fat 83.9g, of which saturates 13.6g; Cholesterol 364mg; Calcium 140mg; Fibre 5.6g; Sodium 1217mg.

Courgette fritters with pistou

A wide variety of different organic courgettes are available, ranging in colour from pale yellow to deep green. The pistou sauce, made with fresh basil, provides a lovely contrast in flavour.

SERVES 4

450g/1lb courgettes (zucchini), grated
75g/3oz/²/₃ cup plain (all-purpose) or
    wholemeal (whole-wheat) flour
1 egg, separated
15ml/1 tbsp olive oil
oil for shallow frying
sea salt and ground black pepper

FOR THE PISTOU SAUCE

15g/¹/₂oz/¹/₂ cup basil leaves
4 garlic cloves, crushed
90g/3¹/₂oz/1 cup finely grated Parmesan
    cheese or premium Italian-style
    vegetarian cheese
finely grated rind of 1 lemon
150ml/¹/₄ pint/²/₃ cup olive oil

1 To make the pistou sauce, use a mortar and pestle to crush the basil leaves and garlic to a fine paste. Transfer to a bowl and stir in the grated cheese and lemon rind. Gradually blend in the oil until combined. Transfer to a serving dish.

2 To make the fritters, sprinkle the grated courgettes with plenty of salt and leave in a sieve (strainer) over a bowl for 1 hour. Rinse thoroughly and dry on kitchen paper.

3 Sift the flour into a bowl. Make a well in the centre, then add the egg yolk and oil. Measure 75ml/5 tbsp water and add a little to the bowl. Whisk the egg yolk and oil, gradually incorporating the flour and water to make a smooth batter. Season and set aside for 30 minutes.

4 Stir the courgettes into the batter. Whisk the egg white until stiff, then fold into the batter.

5 Heat 1cm/¹/₂in of oil in a frying pan. Add dessertspoons of batter and fry for 2 minutes until golden brown and crispy. Remove from the pan, using a slotted spoon. Place on kitchen paper while frying the rest. Serve with the pistou sauce.

Nutritional information per portion: Energy 207kcal/857kJ; Protein 8.3g; Carbohydrate 10.8g, of which sugars 4.7g; Fat 14.8g, of which saturates 2.4g; Cholesterol 95mg; Calcium 104mg; Fibre 2.1g; Sodium 50mg.

Grilled aubergine parcels

This is a great organic recipe – little Italian bundles of tomatoes, mozzarella cheese and basil, wrapped in slices of aubergine. The parcels are naturally low in saturated fat, sugar and salt.

SERVES 4

2 large, long aubergines (eggplant)
225g/8oz buffalo mozzarella cheese
2 plum tomatoes
16 large basil leaves
30ml/2 tbsp olive oil
sea salt and ground black pepper

FOR THE DRESSING

60ml/4 tbsp olive oil
5ml/1 tsp balsamic vinegar
15ml/1 tbsp sun-dried tomato
     purée (paste)
15ml/1 tbsp lemon juice

FOR THE GARNISH

30ml/2 tbsp toasted pine nuts
torn basil leaves

1 Remove the stalks from the aubergines and then cut them lengthways into 16 thin, even slices (each about 5mm/¼ in thick). Disregard the first and last.

2 Boil the aubergine slices in water for 2 minutes. Drain, then dry on kitchen paper. Cut the mozzarella cheese into eight slices. Cut each tomato into eight slices, not counting the first and last slices.

3 Place two aubergine slices on a flameproof tray, in a cross. Place a slice of tomato in the centre, season lightly, add a basil leaf, then a slice of mozzarella, another basil leaf, a slice of tomato and more seasoning.

4 Fold the ends of the aubergine slices around the mozzarella and tomato filling to make a parcel. Repeat to make eight parcels. Chill them for 20 minutes.

5 To make the dressing, whisk together the ingredients and season.

6 Preheat the grill (broiler). Brush the parcels with oil and cook for 5 minutes on each side. Serve hot, with the dressing, sprinkled with pine nuts and basil.

Nutritional information per portion: Energy 350kcal/1449kJ; Protein 12.7g; Carbohydrate 5g, of which sugars 4.7g; Fat 31.2g, of which saturates 10.5g; Cholesterol 33mg; Calcium 223mg; Fibre 3.6g; Sodium 230mg.

Spiced vegetable couscous

This tasty vegetarian main course is easy to make and can be prepared with any number of seasonal organic vegetables such as spinach, peas, broad beans or corn.

SERVES 6

45ml/3 tbsp olive oil
1 large onion, finely chopped
2 garlic cloves, crushed
15ml/1 tbsp tomato purée (paste)
2.5ml/¹/₂ tsp ground turmeric
2.5ml/¹/₂ tsp cayenne pepper
5ml/1 tsp ground coriander
5ml/1 tsp ground cumin
225g/8oz/1¹/₂ cups cauliflower florets
225g/8oz baby carrots, trimmed
1 red (bell) pepper, seeded and diced
225g/8oz courgettes (zucchini), sliced
400g/14oz can chickpeas
4 beefsteak tomatoes, skinned and sliced
45ml/3 tbsp chopped fresh coriander
sea salt and ground black pepper
coriander sprigs, to garnish
2.5ml/¹/₂ tsp sea salt
450g/1lb/2²/₃ cups couscous
50g/2oz/¹/₄ cup butter or 50ml/3¹/₂ tbsp
    sunflower oil

1 Heat 30ml/2 tbsp oil in a large pan, add the onion and garlic and cook until soft and translucent. Stir in the tomato purée, turmeric, cayenne, coriander and cumin. Cook, stirring, for 2 minutes.

2 Add the cauliflower, baby carrots and pepper, with enough water to come halfway up the vegetables. Bring to the boil, lower the heat, cover and simmer for 10 minutes. Add the courgettes, the drained and rinsed chickpeas and tomatoes to the pan and cook for 10 minutes. Stir in the fresh coriander and season. Keep hot.

3 To cook the couscous, bring about 475ml/16fl oz/2 cups water to the boil in a large pan. Add the remaining olive oil and the salt. Remove from the heat and add the couscous, stirring. Allow to swell for 2 minutes.

4 Add the butter or sunflower oil. Heat gently, stirring to separate the grains.

5 Turn the couscous out on to a warm serving dish, and spoon the vegetables on top, pouring over any liquid. Garnish with coriander and serve immediately.

Nutritional information per portion: Energy 382kcal/1597kJ; Protein 13.3g; Carbohydrate 63g, of which sugars 12.4g; Fat 10g, of which saturates 1.3g; Cholesterol 0mg; Calcium 108mg; Fibre 7.1g; Sodium 187mg.

Grilled vegetable pizza

You really can't go too far wrong with this classic mixture of Mediterranean grilled vegetables on home-made pizza dough. It is filling and healthy, and is a favourite with children.

SERVES 6

1 courgette (zucchini), sliced
2 baby aubergines (eggplant) or 1 small
    aubergine, sliced
30ml/2 tbsp olive oil
1 yellow (bell) pepper, seeded and sliced
115g/4oz/1 cup cornmeal
50g/2oz/¹/₂ cup potato flour
50g/2oz/¹/₂ cup soya flour
5ml/1 tsp baking powder
2.5ml/¹/₂ tsp sea salt
50g/2oz/¹/₄ cup butter or
    non-hydrogenated margarine
about 105ml/7 tbsp milk
4 plum tomatoes, skinned and chopped
30ml/2 tbsp chopped fresh basil
115g/4oz buffalo mozzarella
    cheese, sliced
sea salt and ground black pepper
fresh basil sprigs, to garnish

1 Brush the courgette and aubergine slices with a little oil and place on a grill (broiler) rack with the pepper slices. Grill (broil) until lightly browned, turning once.

2 Heat the oven to 200°C/400°F/Gas 6. Place the cornmeal, potato flour, soya flour, baking powder and salt in a mixing bowl and stir to mix. Lightly rub in the margarine until the mixture resembles coarse breadcrumbs, then stir in enough of the milk to make a soft but not sticky dough.

3 On a sheet of baking parchment on a baking sheet, gently press the dough out to form a 25cm/10in round, slightly thicker at the edges than at the centre. Lightly brush the dough with any remaining oil, then spread the chopped plum tomatoes evenly over the dough.

4 Sprinkle with the chopped basil and season with salt and pepper. Arrange the grilled (broiled) vegetables over the tomatoes and top with the cheese.

5 Bake for 25–30 minutes until crisp and golden brown. Garnish the pizza with fresh basil sprigs and serve immediately, cut into slices.

Nutritional information per portion: Energy 400kcal/1666kJ; Protein 11.9g; Carbohydrate 34.6g, of which sugars 9.6g; Fat 23.9g, of which saturates 5.3g; Cholesterol 18mg; Calcium 166mg; Fibre 4.4g; Sodium 240mg.

Moroccan fish tagine with couscous

With its balance of amino acids and oils, fish is a staple food for the organic cook. Always ensure that it is either organically farmed or sustainably caught in the wild.

SERVES 8

1.3kg/3lb firm fish fillets such as monkfish or
  hoki, skinned and cut into 5cm/2in cubes
60ml/4 tbsp olive oil
4 onions, chopped
1 large aubergine (eggplant), cut into
  1cm/^{1}/$_2$in cubes
2 courgettes (zucchini), cut into
  1cm/^{1}/$_2$in cubes
400g/14oz can chopped tomatoes
400ml/14fl oz/1^2/$_3$ cups passata (bottled
  strained tomatoes)
200ml/7fl oz/scant 1 cup fish stock
1 preserved lemon, chopped
90g/3^1/$_2$oz/scant 1 cup olives

60ml/4 tbsp chopped fresh
  coriander (cilantro)
sea salt and ground black pepper
couscous, to serve
coriander sprigs, to garnish

FOR THE HARISSA
3 large fresh red chillies, seeded and chopped
3 garlic cloves, peeled
15ml/1 tbsp ground coriander
30ml/2 tbsp ground cumin
5ml/1 tsp ground cinnamon
grated rind of 1 lemon
30ml/2 tbsp sunflower oil

1 To make the harissa, whizz everything in a food processor to a smooth paste. Then put the fish in a wide bowl and add 30ml/2 tbsp of the harissa. Toss to coat, cover and chill for at least 1 hour.

2 Heat half the oil in a shallow pan. Cook the onions for 10 minutes. Stir in the remaining harissa; cook for 5 minutes, stirring occasionally. Heat the remaining olive oil in a separate pan. Add the aubergine cubes and fry until golden brown. Add the cubed courgettes and fry for a further 2 minutes, stirring occasionally.

3 Tip the aubergine mixture into the shallow pan and combine with the onions, then stir in the chopped tomatoes, the passata and fish stock. Bring to the boil, then lower the heat and simmer the mixture for about 20 minutes.

4 Stir the fish cubes and preserved lemon into the pan. Add the olives and stir gently. Cover and simmer gently for 15–20 minutes until the fish is just cooked through. Season to taste. Stir in the chopped coriander. Serve with couscous and garnish with coriander sprigs.

Nutritional information per portion: Energy 338kcal/1422kJ; Protein 33.7g; Carbohydrate 24.7g, of which sugars 12.1g; Fat 12.4g, of which saturates 1.8g; Cholesterol 23mg; Calcium 100mg; Fibre 6.6g; Sodium 517mg.

Hake au poivre with red pepper relish

People in Europe should use South African hake rather than hake from European waters, where stocks are low due to overfishing. Or try line-caught tuna or haddock from Icelandic waters.

SERVES 4

30–45ml/2–3 tbsp mixed peppercorns (black, white, pink and green)
4 hake steaks, about 175g/6oz each
30ml/2 tbsp olive oil
sea salt and ground black pepper

FOR THE RELISH
2 red (bell) peppers
15ml/1 tbsp olive oil
2 garlic cloves, chopped

4 ripe tomatoes, peeled, seeded and quartered
4 drained canned anchovy fillets, roughly chopped
5ml/1 tsp capers
15ml/1 tbsp balsamic vinegar, plus a little extra to serve
12 fresh basil leaves, shredded, plus a few extra to garnish

1 Coarsely crush the peppercorns with a mortar and pestle. Season the fillets lightly with salt, then coat them evenly on both sides with the crushed peppercorns. Set the coated fish steaks aside while you make the red pepper relish.

2 Cut the red peppers in half lengthways, remove the core and seeds and cut the flesh into 1cm/½in wide strips. Heat the olive oil in a shallow pan with a lid. Add the peppers and stir until slightly softened. Stir in the chopped garlic, tomatoes and anchovies, cover the pan and simmer very gently for 20 minutes until the peppers are very soft.

3 Tip the contents of the pan into a food processor and whizz to a coarse purée. Transfer to a bowl and season to taste. Stir in the capers, balsamic vinegar and basil. Keep the relish hot.

4 Heat the olive oil in a shallow pan, add the hake steaks and fry them, in batches if necessary, for 5 minutes on each side, turning them once or twice, until they are just cooked through.

5 Place the fish on individual plates and spoon a little red pepper relish on to each plate. Garnish with basil leaves and a little extra balsamic vinegar. Serve the rest of the relish separately.

Nutritional information per portion: Energy 283kcal/1186kJ; Protein 33.7g; Carbohydrate 8.2g, of which sugars 8g; Fat 13g, of which saturates 1.9g; Cholesterol 42mg; Calcium 47mg; Fibre 2.3g; Sodium 304mg.

Fresh tuna salad Niçoise

Make this classic salad something really special by using fresh tuna. When buying tuna, make sure it is line-caught tuna, certified by the international Marine Stewardship Council (MSC).

SERVES 4

4 tuna steaks, about 150g/5oz each
30ml/2 tbsp olive oil
225g/8oz French (green) beans, trimmed
1 small cos or romaine lettuce or 2 Little Gem (Bibb) lettuces
4 new potatoes, boiled
4 ripe tomatoes, or 12 cherry tomatoes
2 red (bell) peppers, seeded and cut into thin strips
4 hard-boiled eggs, sliced
8 drained anchovy fillets in oil, halved lengthways (optional)
16 large black olives
sea salt and ground black pepper
12 fresh basil leaves, to garnish

FOR THE DRESSING
15ml/1 tbsp red wine vinegar
90ml/6 tbsp olive oil
1 fat garlic clove, crushed

1 Brush the tuna on both sides with a little olive oil and season. Heat a ridged griddle or the grill (broiler) until very hot, then grill (broil) the steaks for 1–2 minutes each side until pink and juicy in the middle.

2 Cook the beans in a pan of lightly salted boiling water for 4–5 minutes. Drain, refresh under cold water and drain again.

3 Separate the lettuce leaves and rinse thoroughly with cold water. Dry on kitchen paper and arrange them on four serving plates.

4 Slice the cooked potatoes and tomatoes (leave cherry tomatoes whole) and divide among the plates. Arrange the beans and red pepper strips on top.

5 Shell the hard-boiled eggs and cut them into thick slices. Place a few slices of egg on each plate with the anchovy fillets, if using, and olives.

6 To make the dressing, whisk together the vinegar, olive oil and garlic and season to taste. Drizzle over the salads, arrange the tuna steaks on top, scatter over the basil and serve.

Nutritional information per portion: Energy 578kcal/2408kJ; Protein 46.4g; Carbohydrate 15g, of which sugars 10.6g; Fat 37.5g, of which saturates 7.1g; Cholesterol 235mg; Calcium 127mg; Fibre 4.7g; Sodium 585mg.

Griddled chicken with tomato salsa

This simple meal is a great way to enjoy the flavour, colour and health benefits of organic ingredients. For the best result, marinate the chicken overnight.

SERVES 4

4 boneless, skinless chicken breast fillets,
    about 175g/6oz each
30ml/2 tbsp fresh lemon juice
30ml/2 tbsp olive oil
10ml/2 tsp ground cumin
10ml/2 tsp dried oregano
15ml/1 tbsp coarse black pepper

FOR THE SALSA

1 green chilli
450g/1lb plum tomatoes, seeded
    and chopped
3 spring onions (scallions), chopped
15ml/1 tbsp chopped fresh parsley
30ml/2 tbsp chopped fresh
    coriander (cilantro)
30ml/2 tbsp fresh lemon juice
45ml/3 tbsp olive oil

1 With a meat mallet, pound the chicken between two sheets of clear film (plastic wrap) until thin.

2 In a shallow dish, mix the lemon juice, oil, cumin, oregano and pepper. Add the chicken and turn to coat. Cover and leave to marinate in the refrigerator for 2 hours or overnight.

3 To make the salsa, char the chilli skin over a gas flame or under the grill (broiler). Cool for 5 minutes. Carefully rub off the charred skin. For a less hot flavour, discard the seeds.

4 Chop the chilli very finely and place in a bowl. Add the seeded and chopped tomatoes, the chopped spring onions, chopped fresh parsley and coriander, lemon juice and olive oil and mix well. Set aside until ready to serve.

5 Remove the chicken from the marinade. Heat a ridged griddle. Add the chicken fillets and cook on one side until browned, for about 3 minutes. Turn over and cook for a further 4 minutes. Serve with the chilli salsa.

Nutritional information per portion: Energy 260kcal/1096kJ; Protein 43.3g; Carbohydrate 4.1g, of which sugars 4g; Fat 8g, of which saturates 1.4g; Cholesterol 123mg; Calcium 45mg; Fibre 1.9g; Sodium 120mg.

Grilled skewered chicken

Organic chicken has a superb flavour and these fabulous little skewers make great finger food. Cook on the barbecue or grill and serve sizzling hot.

SERVES 4

8 chicken thighs with skin, boned
8 large, thick spring onions
    (scallions), trimmed
oil, for greasing
lemon wedges, to serve

FOR THE YAKITORI SAUCE
60ml/4 tbsp sake
75ml/5 tbsp shoyu
15ml/1 tbsp mirin
15ml/1 tbsp unrefined caster (superfine)
    sugar or rapadura

1 First, make the yakitori sauce. Mix all the ingredients together in a small pan. Bring to the boil, then reduce the heat and simmer for 10 minutes.

2 Cut the chicken into 2.5cm/1in cubes. Cut the spring onions into 2.5cm/1in long sticks.

3 To cook the chicken on a barbecue, soak eight bamboo skewers overnight in water to prevent them burning during cooking. Prepare the barbecue. Thread about four pieces of chicken and three spring onion pieces on to each of the skewers. Place the yakitori sauce in a small bowl and have a brush ready.

4 Cook the skewered chicken on the barbecue. Keep the skewer handles away from the fire, turning them frequently. Brush the chicken with sauce. Return to the coals and repeat this process twice more until the chicken is well cooked.

5 Alternatively, to grill (broil), preheat the grill (broiler) to high. Oil the wire rack and spread out the chicken cubes on it. Grill both sides of the chicken until the juices drip, then dip the pieces in the sauce and put back on the rack. Grill for 30 seconds on each side, repeating the dipping process twice more.

6 Set aside and keep warm. Gently grill the spring onions until soft and slightly brown outside. Do not dip. Thread the chicken and spring onion pieces on to skewers as above.

7 Arrange the chicken and spring onions on a serving platter. Serve accompanied by lemon wedges.

Nutritional information per portion: Energy 165kcal/695kJ; Protein 22g; Carbohydrate 9g, of which sugars 8.8g; Fat 2.9g, of which saturates 0.8g; Cholesterol 105mg; Calcium 24mg; Fibre 0.4g; Sodium 1429mg.

Olive oil roasted chicken with summer vegetables

This is a delicious alternative to a traditional roast chicken. Organic chicken can be so much tastier and more tender than intensively reared poultry, especially if the birds are raised biodynamically.

SERVES 4

1.8–2kg/4–4¹/₂lb roasting chicken
150ml/¹/₄ pint/²/₃ cup extra virgin
    olive oil
¹/₂ lemon
few sprigs of fresh thyme
450g/1lb small new potatoes
1 aubergine (eggplant), cut into
    2.5cm/1in cubes
1 red (bell) pepper, seeded and quartered
1 fennel bulb, trimmed and quartered
8 large garlic cloves, unpeeled
coarse sea salt and ground black pepper

1 Heat the oven to 200°C/400°F/Gas 6. Rub the chicken all over with olive oil and season with pepper. Place the lemon half inside the bird, with a sprig or two of thyme. Put the chicken breast side down in a large roasting pan. Roast for 30 minutes.

2 Remove from the oven and season with salt. Turn right side up and baste. Surround with the potatoes, rolling them in the pan juices. Return to the oven.

3 After 30 minutes, add the aubergine, red pepper, fennel and garlic cloves to the pan. Drizzle with the remaining oil, and season with salt and pepper. Add any remaining thyme to the vegetables. Return to the oven, and cook for about 40 minutes more, basting and turning the vegetables occasionally.

4 Push the tip of a sharp knife between the thigh and breast. If the juices run clear, the bird is done. The vegetables should be tender and beginning to brown. Serve from the pan, or transfer the vegetables to a serving dish, and joint the chicken and place it on top. Serve the skimmed juices in a gravy boat.

Nutritional information per portion: Energy 713kcal/2973kJ; Protein 51.2g; Carbohydrate 39.3g, of which sugars 13g; Fat 40g, of which saturates 12.9g; Cholesterol 261mg; Calcium 103mg; Fibre 5.4g; Sodium 250mg.

Thai beef salad

Meat does not need to dominate a meal, as this light Thai salad shows. Especially when cooking with good-quality organic meat, a little adds a lot of flavour.

SERVES 4

675g/1¹/₂lb fillet (tenderloin) or rump
   (round) beef steak
30ml/2 tbsp olive oil
225g/8oz/3¹/₄ cups shiitake mushrooms
2 small mild red chillies, seeded and sliced

FOR THE DRESSING

3 spring onions (scallions), finely chopped
2 garlic cloves, finely chopped
juice of 1 lime
15–30ml/1–2 tbsp fish or oyster sauce
5ml/1 tsp unrefined soft light brown
   sugar or rapadura
30ml/2 tbsp chopped coriander (cilantro)

TO SERVE

1 cos or romaine lettuce, torn into strips
175g/6oz cherry tomatoes, halved
5cm/2in piece cucumber, peeled, halved
   and thinly sliced
45ml/3 tbsp toasted sesame seeds

1 Preheat the grill (broiler) until hot, then cook the steak for 2–4 minutes on each side, depending on how well done you like steak. (In Thailand, the beef is traditionally served quite rare.) Leave the beef to cool for at least 15 minutes.

2 Use a very sharp knife to slice the meat as thinly as possible and place the slices in a bowl.

3 Heat the olive oil in a small frying pan. Finely slice the mushrooms and add them with the seeded and sliced red chillies and cook for 5 minutes, stirring occasionally. Turn off the heat and add the grilled steak slices to the pan, then stir well to coat the beef slices thoroughly in the cooked chilli and mushroom mixture.

4 Stir all the ingredients for the dressing together, then pour it over the meat mixture and toss gently.

5 Arrange the salad ingredients on a serving plate. Spoon the warm steak mixture in the centre and sprinkle the sesame seeds over. Serve at once.

Nutritional information per portion: Energy 381kcal/1591kJ; Protein 39.8g; Carbohydrate 4.1g, of which sugars 3.8g; Fat 23g, of which saturates 6.6g; Cholesterol 103mg; Calcium 105mg; Fibre 2.5g; Sodium 352mg.

Marinated beef with onion rings

Mexican chillies combine well with garlic in this marinade for grilled steak. Organic beef is tastier and has a better balance of cholesterol than the non-organic kind.

SERVES 4

20g/3/4oz large mild dried red chillies (such
    as mulato or pasilla)
2 garlic cloves, plain or smoked, finely chopped
5ml/1 tsp ground toasted cumin seeds
5ml/1 tsp dried oregano
60ml/4 tbsp olive oil
4 x 175–225g/6–8oz beef steaks, rump
    (round) or rib-eye
sea salt and ground black pepper

FOR THE ONION RINGS

2 onions, sliced into rings
250ml/8fl oz/1 cup milk or soya milk
75g/3oz/³/₄ cup coarse cornmeal
2.5ml/¹/₂ tsp dried red chilli flakes
5ml/1 tsp ground toasted cumin seeds
5ml/1 tsp dried oregano
sunflower or safflower oil, for deep-frying

1 Cut the stalks from the chillies and discard the seeds. Toast them in a dry frying pan over a high heat, stirring constantly, for 2–4 minutes. Place in a bowl, cover with warm water and leave for 20–30 minutes. Drain and reserve the water.

2 Process the soaked, drained chillies to a paste with the finely chopped garlic, toasted cumin seeds, oregano and oil in a food processor. Add a little of the soaking water, if needed. Season with ground black pepper.

3 Wash and dry the steaks, place them in a non-metallic container, rub the chilli paste all over them and leave to marinate in the refrigerator for up to 12 hours.

4 Soak the onion slices in the milk for 30 minutes. Mix the cornmeal, chilli, cumin and oregano, and season with salt and pepper. Heat the oil for deep-frying in a deep pan to 160–180°C/325–350°F. Drain the rings and coat them in the cornmeal mixture. Fry for 2–4 minutes until brown and crisp. Don't crowd the pan, but cook in batches. Lift the rings out with a slotted spoon and drain on kitchen paper.

5 Heat a barbecue or cast-iron griddle. Season the steaks with salt and cook for about 4 minutes on each side for a medium result; reduce or increase this time according to how rare or well done you like steak. Serve with the onion rings.

Nutritional information per portion: Energy 428kcal/1787kJ; Protein 44.2g; Carbohydrate 17.4g, of which sugars 3g; Fat 20g, of which saturates 5.4g; Cholesterol 91mg; Calcium 51mg; Fibre 0.8g; Sodium 136mg.

Frozen melon

Freezing sorbet in hollowed-out fruit, which is then cut into icy wedges, is an excellent idea. The refreshing flavour makes this dessert irresistible on a hot summer's day.

SERVES 6

50g/2oz/¹⁄₄ cup unrefined caster (superfine)
   sugar or rapadura
30ml/2 tbsp clear honey
15ml/1 tbsp lemon juice
60ml/4 tbsp water

1 medium cantaloupe melon or Charentais
   melon, about 1 kg/2¹⁄₄lb
crushed ice, cucumber slices and borage
   flowers, to decorate

1 Put the sugar, honey, lemon juice and water in a heavy pan, and heat gently until the sugar dissolves. Bring to the boil, and boil for 1 minute, without stirring, to make a syrup. Leave to cool.

2 Cut the cantaloupe or Charentais melon in half and discard the seeds. Carefully scoop out the flesh using a metal spoon or melon baller and place in a food processor, taking care to keep the halved shells intact.

3 Blend the melon flesh until very smooth, then transfer to a mixing bowl. Stir in the cooled sugar syrup and chill until very cold. Invert the melon shells and leave them to drain on kitchen paper for a few minutes, then transfer them to the freezer while making the sorbet.

4 If making by hand, pour the mixture into a container and freeze for 3–4 hours, beating well twice with a fork, a whisk or in a food processor, to break up the ice crystals and produce a smooth texture. If using an ice cream maker, churn the melon mixture in the ice cream maker until the sorbet holds its shape.

5 Pack the sorbet into the melon shells and level the surface with a knife. Use a dessertspoon to scoop out the centre of each filled melon shell to simulate the seed cavity. Freeze the prepared fruit overnight until firm.

6 To serve, use a large knife to cut each melon half into three wedges. Serve on a bed of ice on a large platter or individual serving plates, and decorate with the cucumber slices and borage flowers.

Nutritional information per portion: Energy 67kcal/288kJ; Protein 0.6g; Carbohydrate 16.6g, of which sugars 16.6g; Fat 0.3g, of which saturates 0.1g; Cholesterol 0mg; Calcium 12mg; Fibre 0.1g; Sodium 3mg.

Chocolate meringues with mixed fruit compote

Mini-chocolate meringues are sandwiched with crème fraîche and served with a compote of organic mixed summer berries to make this impressive dessert.

SERVES 6

105ml/7 tbsp unsweetened red grape juice
105ml/7 tbsp unsweetened apple juice
30ml/2 tbsp clear honey
450g/1lb/4 cups mixed fresh summer
    berries, such as blackcurrants, red-
    currants, raspberries and blackberries

FOR THE MERINGUES
3 egg whites
175g/6oz/³/₄ cup unrefined caster
    (superfine) sugar or rapadura
75g/3oz good-quality plain chocolate,
    finely grated
175g/6oz/scant 1 cup crème fraîche

1 Heat the oven to 110°C/225°F/Gas ¼. Grease and line two large baking sheets with baking parchment, cut to fit.

2 To make the meringues, whisk the egg whites in a large mixing bowl until stiff. Gradually whisk in half the sugar, then fold in the remaining sugar, using a metal spoon. Gently fold in the grated plain chocolate.

3 Carefully spoon the meringue mixture into a large piping (pastry) bag fitted with a large star nozzle. Pipe small round whirls of the mixture on to the prepared baking sheets.

4 Bake the meringues for 2¹/₂–3 hours until firm and crisp. Remove from the oven. Carefully peel the meringues off the paper. Transfer to a wire rack to cool.

5 To make the compote, heat the fruit juices in a small pan with the honey until almost boiling. Put the mixed fresh berries in a large bowl and pour over the hot fruit juice and honey mixture. Stir gently to mix, then leave to cool. Cover the bowl with clear film (plastic wrap) and chill.

6 When ready to serve, gently sandwich the cold meringues together with the crème fraîche and arrange them on a serving plate or dish. Serve immediately on individual plates with the fruit compote.

Nutritional information per portion: Energy 343kcal/1442kJ; Protein 4g; Carbohydrate 50.?g, of which sugars 50g; Fat 15.4g, of which saturates 10.1g; Cholesterol 34mg; Calcium 61mg; Fibre 2.2g; Sodium 44mg.

Fragrant fruit salad

Organic summer fruits make a delicious seasonal fruit salad. Any combination of fruits can be used, although this exotic choice is particularly suitable for a dinner party.

SERVES 6

130g/4¹/₂oz/scant ³/₄ cup unrefined
    sugar or rapadura
thinly pared rind and juice of 1 lime
60ml/4 tbsp brandy
5ml/1 tsp instant coffee granules or
    powder dissolved in 30ml/2 tbsp
    boiling water
1 small pineapple
1 papaya
2 pomegranates
1 medium mango
2 passion fruits or kiwi fruit
fine strips of lime peel, to decorate

1 Put the sugar and lime rind in a small pan with 150ml/¹/₄ pint/²/₃ cup water. Heat gently until the sugar dissolves, then bring to the boil and simmer for 5 minutes. Leave to cool, then strain into a large serving bowl, discarding the lime rind. Stir in the lime juice, brandy and dissolved coffee.

2 Using a sharp knife, cut the plume and stalk ends from the pineapple. Peel and cut the flesh into bitesize pieces. Add to the bowl. Discard the central core.

3 Halve the papaya and scoop out the seeds. Cut away the skin, then slice the papaya. Halve the pomegranates and scoop out the seeds. Add to the bowl.

4 Cut the mango lengthways into three pieces, along each side of the stone. Peel the skin off the flesh. Cut into chunks and add to the bowl.

5 Halve the passion fruits and scoop out the flesh or peel and chop the kiwi fruit. Add to the bowl and serve, decorated with lime peel.

Nutritional information per portion: Energy 146kcal/620kJ; Protein 1g; Carbohydrate 33.2g, of which sugars 33.2g; Fat 0.3g, of which saturates 0g; Cholesterol 0mg; Calcium 40mg; Fibre 2.9g; Sodium 7mg.

Summer berries in warm sabayon glaze

This luxurious combination of summer berries under a light and fluffy alcoholic sauce is lightly grilled to form a crisp, caramelized topping.

SERVES 4

450g/1lb/4 cups mixed summer berries, or soft fruit

4 egg yolks

50g/2oz/¼ cup unrefined caster (superfine) sugar or rapadura

120ml/4fl oz/½ cup white dessert wine, plus extra to serve (optional)

a little unrefined icing (confectioners') sugar, sifted, and mint leaves, to decorate (optional)

1 Arrange the fruit in four flameproof dishes. Preheat the grill (broiler).

2 Whisk the egg yolks in a large bowl with the sugar and wine. Place the bowl over a pan of hot water and whisk constantly until thick, fluffy and pale.

3 Pour equal quantities of the sabayon sauce into each dish. Place under the grill for 1–2 minutes until just turning brown. Sprinkle the fruit with icing sugar and scatter with mint leaves just before serving, if you like. Add an extra splash of wine to the dishes, if you like.

Nutritional information per portion: Energy 235kcal/984kJ; Protein 3.9g; Carbohydrate 27.1g, of which sugars 27.1g; Fat 5.6g, of which saturates 1.6g; Cholesterol 202mg; Calcium 48mg; Fibre 1.2g; Sodium 18mg.

Coffee crêpes with peaches and cream

Juicy golden organic peaches and cream conjure up the sweet taste of summer. Here, they are delicious as the filling for these light coffee-flavoured buckwheat crêpes.

SERVES 6

75g/3oz/⅔ cup plain (all-purpose) flour
25g/1oz/¼ cup buckwheat flour
1 egg, beaten
200ml/7fl oz/scant 1 cup milk or soya milk
15g/½oz/1 tbsp butter, melted
100ml/3½fl oz/scant ½ cup brewed
   coffee, cooled
sunflower oil, for frying

FOR THE FILLING
6 ripe peaches
300ml/½ pint/1¼ cups double
   (heavy) cream
15ml/1 tbsp brandy
225g/8oz/1 cup crème fraîche
65g/2½oz/generous ¼ cup unrefined
   caster (superfine) sugar or rapadura
30ml/2 tbsp unrefined icing (confectioners')
   sugar, for dusting (optional)

1 Sift the flours into a mixing bowl. Make a well in the middle and add the beaten egg, half the milk and the melted butter. Gradually mix in the flour, beating until the mixture is smooth. Beat in the remaining milk and the coffee.

2 Heat a drizzle of sunflower oil in a 15–20cm/6–8in crêpe pan. Pour in just enough batter to cover the base of the pan thinly, swirling the pan to spread the mixture evenly. Cook for 2–3 minutes until the underneath is golden brown, then flip the crêpe over using a metal spatula and cook the other side.

3 Slide the crêpe out of the pan on to a plate. Continue making crêpes until you have used up all of the mixture, stacking and interleaving them with baking parchment.

4 To make the filling, halve the peaches and carefully remove the stones. Cut the peaches into thick slices. Whip the cream and brandy together until soft peaks form. Beat the crème fraîche with the sugar until smooth. Beat 30ml/2 tbsp of the cream into the crème fraîche, then fold in the remainder.

5 Place six of the crêpes on individual serving plates. Spoon a little of the brandy cream on to one half of each crêpe and top with peach slices. Gently fold the crêpe over and dust with a little sifted icing sugar, if you like. Serve immediately.

Nutritional information per portion: Energy 578kcal/2403kJ; Protein 6.5g; Carbohydrate 36.3g, of which sugars 23.1g; Fat 45.7g, of which saturates 28.8g; Cholesterol 150mg; Calcium 123mg; Fibre 2.1g; Sodium 63mg.

Blueberry frangipane flan

A tangy lemon pastry case is filled with a nutty sweet almond filling dotted with ripe organic blueberries. Their wonderful colour and taste are a seasonal favourite.

SERVES 6

175g/6oz/1¹/₂ cups plain
   (all-purpose) flour
115g/4oz/¹/₂ cup unsalted (sweet)
   butter or non-hydrogenated margarine
25g/1oz/2 tbsp unrefined caster sugar
   or rapadura
finely grated rind of ¹/₂ lemon
15ml/1 tbsp chilled water
30ml/2 tbsp ground coffee
45ml/3 tbsp milk or soya milk
50g/2oz/¹/₄ cup unsalted (sweet) butter
50g/2oz/¹/₄ cup unrefined caster
   (superfine) sugar or rapadura
1 egg
115g/4oz/1 cup ground almonds
15ml/1 tbsp plain (all-purpose) flour
225g/8oz/2 cups blueberries
30ml/2 tbsp jam
15ml/1 tbsp brandy
crème fraîche or sour cream, to serve

1 Heat the oven to 190°C/375°F/Gas 5. Sift the flour into a bowl and rub in the butter. Stir in the sugar and lemon rind, then add the water and mix to a firm dough. Wrap in clear film (plastic wrap) and chill for 20 minutes.

2 Roll out the pastry on a lightly floured work surface and use to line a 23cm/9in loose-based flan tin (pan). Line the pastry with baking parchment and baking beans and bake for 10 minutes. Remove the paper and beans and bake for a further 10 minutes. Remove from the oven.

3 Bring the milk almost to the boil, then pour over the coffee in a bowl and leave for 4 minutes. Cream the butter and sugar until pale. Beat in the egg, then add the almonds and flour. Strain in the coffee-flavoured milk and fold in.

4 Spoon the coffee mixture evenly into the pastry case. Scatter the blueberries on top, pushing them down slightly into the mixture. Bake for 30 minutes, until firm, covering with foil after 20 minutes. Remove from the oven and cool slightly. Melt the jam and brandy in a small pan. Brush over the flan and remove from the tin. Serve warm with crème fraîche or sour cream.

Nutritional information per portion: Energy 523kcal/2180kJ; Protein 8.9g; Carbohydrate 44.9g, of which sugars 20.2g; Fat 34.8g, of which saturates 15.6g; Cholesterol 91mg; Calcium 132mg; Fibre 3.6g; Sodium 188mg.

Blueberry muffins

Light and fruity, these well-known American muffins are delicious at any time of day. Serve them warm for breakfast or brunch, or as a tea-time treat.

MAKES 12

180g/6¼oz/generous 1½ cups plain
  (all-purpose) flour
60g/2¼oz/¼ cup unrefined sugar
  or rapadura
10ml/2 tsp baking powder
2 eggs
50g/2oz/¼ cup butter or non-
  hydrogenated margarine, melted
175ml/6fl oz/¾ cup milk or soya milk
5ml/1 tsp vanilla extract
5ml/1 tsp grated lemon rind
175g/6oz/1½ cups fresh blueberries

1 Preheat the oven to 200°C/400°F/Gas 6. Grease a 12-cup muffin tin (pan) or arrange 12 paper muffin cases on a baking tray.

2 Sift the plain flour, sugar and baking powder into a large mixing bowl. In another bowl, whisk the eggs until blended. Add the melted butter, milk, vanilla extract and grated lemon rind, and stir thoroughly to combine.

3 Make a well in the dry ingredients and pour in the egg mixture. With a large metal spoon, stir until the flour is just moistened, but not smooth.

4 Add the blueberries to the muffin mixture and gently fold in, being careful not to crush the berries.

5 Spoon the batter into the muffin tin or paper cases, leaving enough room for the muffins to rise. Bake for 20–25 minutes until the tops spring back when touched lightly. Leave the muffins in the tin, if using, for about 5 minutes before turning out on to a wire rack to cool a little before serving.

Nutritional information per portion: Energy 236kcal/992kJ; Protein 4.9g; Carbohydrate 34.7g, of which sugars 12.4g; Fat 9.6g, of which saturates 5.6g; Cholesterol 54mg; Calcium 88mg; Fibre 1.4g; Sodium 92mg.

Apricot and almond tart

This rich tart relies on a simple but perfect combination of apricots and almond filling. Fresh apricots are only available during the summer months, so make the most of them.

SERVES 6

115g/4oz/¹/₂ cup butter or
   non-hydrogenated margarine
115g/4oz/scant ¹/₂ cup unrefined caster
   (superfine) sugar or rapadura
1 egg, beaten
50g/2oz/¹/₃ cup ground rice
50g/2oz/¹/₂ cup ground almonds
few drops of almond extract
450g/1lb fresh apricots, halved and stoned
sifted unrefined icing (confectioners') sugar,
   for dusting (optional)

apricot slices and fresh mint sprigs, to
   decorate (optional)

FOR THE PASTRY
115g/4oz/1 cup brown rice flour
115g/4oz/1 cup cornmeal
115g/4oz/¹/₂ cup butter or
   non-hydrogenated margarine
25g/1oz/2 tbsp unrefined caster (superfine)
   sugar or rapadura
1 egg yolk

1 To make the pastry, place the rice flour and cornmeal in a large mixing bowl and stir to mix. Lightly rub in the butter or margarine with your fingertips until the mixture resembles fine breadcrumbs.

2 Add the sugar, the egg yolk and enough chilled water to make a smooth, soft but not sticky dough. Wrap in clear film (plastic wrap) and chill for 30 minutes.

3 Heat the oven to 180°C/350°F/Gas 4. Line a 24cm/9¹/₂in loose-bottomed flan tin (pan) with the pastry by pressing it gently over the base and up the sides, making sure that there are no gaps. Trim the edge with a knife.

4 In a mixing bowl, cream together the butter or margarine and sugar, using a wooden spoon, until the mixture is light and fluffy. Gradually add the beaten egg, beating well each time. Fold in the ground rice, almonds and almond extract, and mix well.

5 Spoon the almond mixture into the pastry case, spreading it evenly with the back of a spoon, then arrange the apricot halves cut side down on top.

6 Place the tart on a baking sheet and bake for 40–45 minutes until the filling and pastry are lightly browned. Serve warm or cold, dusted with icing sugar and decorated with apricots and sprigs of mint.

Nutritional information per portion: Energy 640kcal/2670kJ; Protein 8.4g; Carbohydrate 66.2g, of which sugars 30.7g; Fat 39g, of which saturates 20.9g; Cholesterol 147mg; Calcium 89mg; Fibre 3.1g; Sodium 251mg.

Autumn

As the nights draw in, it's time to make the most of hearty vegetables such as parsnips, squashes and sweet potatoes, and enjoy delicious fish dishes. Apples, plums and pears add flavour to both sweet and savoury dishes, while blackberry and apple soufflés round off dinner parties perfectly. Freshly baked cakes – served straight from the oven – are especially satisfying.

Roast garlic with goat's cheese pâté

The combination of sweet, mellow roasted garlic and goat's cheese is a classic one. The pâté is flavoured with walnuts and herbs and is particularly good made with the new season's walnuts.

SERVES 4

4 large garlic bulbs
4 fresh rosemary sprigs
8 fresh thyme sprigs
60ml/4 tbsp olive oil
sea salt and ground black pepper
thyme sprigs, to garnish
4–8 slices sourdough bread and walnuts,
**   to serve**

FOR THE PÂTÉ

200g/7oz/scant 1 cup soft goat's cheese
5ml/1 tsp finely chopped fresh thyme
15ml/1 tbsp chopped fresh parsley
50g/2oz/¹/₃ cup walnuts, chopped
15ml/1 tbsp walnut oil (optional)
fresh thyme, to garnish

1 Heat the oven to 180°C/350°F/Gas 4. Peel the garlic bulbs and place them in a large ovenproof dish. Tuck in the fresh rosemary and thyme sprigs, drizzle over the olive oil and season with sea salt and plenty of ground black pepper.

2 Cover the garlic tightly with foil and bake in the oven for 50–60 minutes, opening the parcel and basting once halfway through. Leave to cool.

3 Heat the grill (broiler). To make the pâté, cream the cheese with the thyme, parsley and chopped walnuts. Beat in 15ml/1 tbsp of the cooking oil from the garlic and season with black pepper. Transfer to a serving bowl and chill.

4 Brush the sourdough bread slices on one side with the remaining cooking oil from the garlic bulbs, then grill (broil) until lightly toasted.

5 Divide the pâté among four plates. Drizzle the walnut oil, if using, over the goat's cheese pâté and grind some black pepper over it. Place some garlic on each plate and serve with the pâté and toasted bread. Garnish the pâté with a little fresh thyme and serve a few freshly shelled walnuts with each portion.

Nutritional information per portion: Energy 371kcal/1534kJ; Protein 14.5g; Carbohydrate 5.1g, of which sugars 1.3g; Fat 32.7g, of which saturates 11.3g; Cholesterol 47mg; Calcium 91mg; Fibre 1.7g; Sodium 304mg.

Slow-cooked shiitake with shoyu

Organic shiitake mushrooms are so rich and filling that they are known as "vegetarian steak". This Japanese dish, known as fukumé-ni, *can last a few weeks in the refrigerator.*

SERVES 4

20 dried shiitake mushrooms
45ml/3 tbsp sunflower or safflower oil
30ml/2 tbsp shoyu
15ml/1 tbsp toasted sesame oil

1 Start soaking the dried shiitake the day before. Put them in a large bowl almost full of water. Cover the shiitake with a plate or lid to stop them floating to the surface of the water. Leave to soak overnight.

2 Measure 120ml/4fl oz/$^1/_2$ cup liquid from the bowl. Drain the shiitake into a sieve (strainer). Remove and discard the stalks.

3 Heat the oil in a wok or a large frying pan. Stir-fry the shiitake over a high heat for 5 minutes, stirring continuously.

4 Reduce the heat to the lowest setting, then add the measured liquid and the shoyu. Cook the mushrooms until there is almost no moisture left, stirring frequently. Add the toasted sesame oil and remove from the heat.

5 Leave to cool, then slice and arrange the shiitake on a large plate.

Nutritional information per portion: Energy 16kcal/69kJ; Protein 2g; Carbohydrate 1g, of which sugars 0.8g; Fat 0.5g, of which saturates 0.1g; Cholesterol 0mg; Calcium 7mg; Fibre 1.1g; Sodium 539mg.

Red onion and mushroom tartlets with goat's cheese

Crisp and savoury, these attractive little tarts are delicious served with a few mixed salad leaves drizzled with a garlic-infused French dressing.

SERVES 6

60ml/4 tbsp olive oil
25g/1oz/2 tbsp butter or non-
  hydrogenated margarine
4 red onions, thinly sliced
5ml/1 tsp unrefined soft light brown sugar
15ml/1 tbsp balsamic vinegar
15ml/1 tbsp soy sauce
200g/7oz/3 cups button (white)
  mushrooms, sliced
1 garlic clove, finely chopped
2.5ml/1/2 tsp chopped fresh tarragon
30ml/2 tbsp chopped fresh parsley

250g/9oz goat's cheese log (chèvre)
sea salt and ground black pepper
mixed salad leaves, to serve

FOR THE PASTRY
200g/7oz/1³/₄ cups plain (all-purpose) flour
pinch of cayenne pepper
90g/3¹/₂oz/scant ¹/₂ cup butter or non-
  hydrogenated margarine
40g/1¹/₂oz/¹/₂ cup freshly grated Parmesan
  cheese or premium vegetarian cheese
45–60ml/3–4 tbsp iced water

1 To make the pastry, sift the flour and cayenne into a bowl, add the butter, and rub in with the fingertips.

2 Stir in the grated cheese, then bind the pastry with the iced water. Press the pastry into a ball, then wrap it in clear film (plastic wrap) and chill.

3 Heat 15ml/1 tbsp of the oil and half the butter in a heavy frying pan, then add the onions. Cover and cook gently for 15 minutes, stirring occasionally.

4 Uncover the pan, increase the heat slightly and sprinkle in the sugar. Cook, stirring frequently, until the onions begin to caramelize and brown. Add the balsamic vinegar and soy sauce and cook briskly until the liquid evaporates. Season to taste then set aside.

5 Heat another 30ml/2 tbsp of the oil and the remaining butter or margarine in a pan. Add the sliced mushrooms and chopped garlic and cook fairly briskly for 5–6 minutes, or until the mushrooms are browned and cooked.

6 Set a few cooked mushrooms and onion rings aside. Stir the rest of the mushrooms into the onions with the tarragon and parsley. Adjust the seasoning. Heat the oven to 190°C/375°F/Gas 5.

7 Roll out the pastry and use to line six 10cm/4in tartlet tins (pans). Prick the pastry bases with a fork and line the sides with strips of foil. Bake for 10 minutes, remove the foil and bake for another 5–7 minutes, or until the pastry is lightly browned and cooked. Remove the tartlets from the oven and increase the temperature to 200°C/400°F/Gas 6.

8 Remove the pastry shells from the tins and arrange them on a baking sheet. Divide the onion mixture equally among the pastry shells. Cut the goat's cheese into six equal slices and place one slice on each tartlet. Distribute the reserved mushrooms and onion rings, drizzle with the remaining oil and season with pepper.

9 Return the tartlets to the oven and bake for 5–8 minutes, or until the goat's cheese is just beginning to turn brown. Serve with mixed salad leaves.

Nutritional information per portion: Energy 595kcal/2482kJ; Protein 15.4g; Carbohydrate 50.8g, of which sugars 8.1g; Fat 39.3g, of which saturates 5.9g; Cholesterol 74mg; Calcium 139mg; Fibre 1.6g; Sodium 542mg.

Clam, mushroom and potato chowder

Clams are members of the same family as mussels, scallops and oysters. They have a sweet flavour and firm texture, which combine beautifully with wild mushrooms in this filling soup.

SERVES 4

48 clams, scrubbed

50g/2oz/¹/₄ cup unsalted (sweet) butter or non-hydrogenated margarine

1 large onion, chopped

1 celery stick, sliced

1 carrot, sliced

225g/8oz/3³/₄ cups assorted wild and cultivated mushrooms

225g/8oz floury potatoes (such as Maris Piper or King Edward), thickly sliced

1.2 litres/2 pints/5 cups boiling light chicken or vegetable stock

1 thyme sprig

4 parsley stalks

sea salt and ground black pepper

thyme sprigs, to garnish

1 Place the clams in a large, heavy pan, discarding any that are open. Add 1cm/¹/₂in of water to the pan, then cover and bring to the boil. Cook the clams over a medium heat for 6–8 minutes, shaking the pan occasionally, until the clams open (discard any clams that do not open).

2 Drain the clams over a bowl and remove most of the shells, leaving some in the shells as a garnish. Strain the cooking juices into the bowl, add all the clams and set aside.

3 Add the butter, onion, celery and carrot to the pan and cook gently until just softened but not coloured. Add the wild and cultivated mushrooms and cook for 3–4 minutes until their juices begin to appear. Add the potato slices, the clams and their juices, the stock, thyme and parsley stalks.

4 Bring to the boil, then reduce the heat, cover and simmer for 25 minutes. Season to taste, ladle into soup bowls, and garnish with thyme sprigs.

Nutritional information per portion: Energy 203kcal/848kJ; Protein 10.8g; Carbohydrate 15.8g, of which sugars 5.2g; Fat 11.2g, of which saturates 6.8g; Cholesterol 60mg; Calcium 66mg; Fibre 2.4g; Sodium 696mg.

Potatoes and **parsnips baked** with **garlic** and **cream**

As the sweet organic potatoes and parsnips cook, they gradually absorb the garlic-flavoured cream, while the cheese browns to a crispy finish.

SERVES 4–6

3 large potatoes, total weight about
    675g/1½lb
350g/12oz small to medium parsnips
200ml/7fl oz/scant 1 cup single (light)
    cream or soya cream
105ml/7 tbsp milk or soya milk
2 garlic cloves, crushed
butter or olive oil, for greasing
about 5ml/1 tsp freshly grated nutmeg
75g/3oz/¾ cup coarsely grated
    Cheddar cheese
sea salt and ground black pepper

1 Cut the peeled potatoes and parsnips into thin slices. Cook in a steamer for 5 minutes. Leave to cool slightly. In a heavy pan, bring the cream, milk and garlic to the boil over a medium heat. Remove from the heat and leave at room temperature for 10 minutes.

2 Lightly grease a 25cm/10in long, shallow rectangular earthenware baking dish with butter or oil. Heat the oven to 180°C/350°F/Gas 4. Arrange the potatoes and parsnips in layers in the dish, sprinkling each layer with a little freshly grated nutmeg and salt, and plenty of ground black pepper.

3 Pour the garlic, cream and milk mixture into the dish and press the vegetables down so that the liquid is just underneath the top layer. Cover the dish with a piece of lightly buttered foil or baking parchment and bake for 45 minutes.

4 Remove from the oven and remove the foil or paper. Sprinkle the grated Cheddar cheese over the vegetables in an even layer. Return to the oven and bake uncovered for a further 20–30 minutes until the topping is golden brown.

Nutritional information per portion: Energy 241kcal/1012kJ; Protein 7.8g; Carbohydrate 27.2g, of which sugars 6.4g; Fat 11.7g, of which saturates 7.2g; Cholesterol 31mg; Calcium 173mg; Fibre 3.9g; Sodium 126mg.

Roasted garlic and squash soup

This is a wonderful, richly flavoured dish. A spoonful of hot and spicy tomato salsa gives bite to the sweet-tasting butternut squash and garlic soup.

SERVES 4–5

2 garlic bulbs, outer papery skin removed
75ml/5 tbsp olive oil
a few fresh thyme sprigs
1 large butternut squash, halved and seeded
2 onions, chopped
5ml/1 tsp ground coriander
1.2 litres/2 pints/5 cups vegetable or
 chicken stock

30–45ml/2–3 tbsp chopped fresh oregano
 or marjoram
sea salt and ground black pepper

FOR THE SALSA

4 large ripe tomatoes, halved and seeded
1 red (bell) pepper, halved and seeded
1 large fresh red chilli, halved and seeded
30–45ml/2–3 tbsp extra virgin olive oil
15ml/1 tbsp balsamic vinegar

1 Preheat the oven to 220°C/425°F/Gas 7. Place the garlic bulbs on a piece of foil and pour over half of the olive oil. Add the sprigs of thyme, then fold the foil around the garlic bulbs to enclose them completely.

2 Place the foil parcel on a baking sheet with the butternut squash and brush the squash with 15ml/1 tbsp of the remaining olive oil. Add the halved and seeded tomatoes, red pepper and fresh chilli for the salsa.

3 Roast the vegetables for 25 minutes, then remove the tomatoes, pepper and chilli. Reduce the temperature to 190°C/375°F/Gas 5 and cook the squash and garlic for 20–25 minutes more, or until the squash is tender.

4 Heat the remaining oil in a large, heavy pan and cook the onions and ground coriander gently for about 10 minutes, or until softened.

5 Skin the pepper and chilli and process in a food processor or blender with the tomatoes and 30ml/ 2 tbsp olive oil. Stir in the vinegar and seasoning to taste. Add the remaining oil if you think that the salsa needs it.

6 Squeeze the roasted garlic out of its papery skin into the onions. Then, scoop the squash out of its skin and add it to the onions, garlic and coriander in the pan. Next, add the vegetable or chicken stock, 2.5ml/^{1}/2 tsp salt and plenty of black pepper. Bring to the boil and simmer for 10 minutes.

7 Stir in half the chopped fresh oregano or marjoram and allow the soup to cool slightly, then process it, in batches if necessary, in a food processor or blender until smooth. Alternatively, press the soup through a fine sieve (strainer).

8 Reheat the soup in a clean pan without allowing it to boil, then taste for seasoning before ladling it into individual warmed bowls. Top each with a spoonful of the tomato salsa and sprinkle over the remaining chopped fresh oregano or marjoram. Serve immediately.

Nutritional information per portion: Energy 120kcal/502kJ; Protein 5g; Carbohydrate 15.7g, of which sugars 9.1g; Fat 4.6g, of which saturates 0.8g; Cholesterol 0mg; Calcium 70mg; Fibre 4.6g; Sodium 9mg.

Garlic chive rice with mushrooms

There are many varieties of organic mushrooms to choose from. They all combine well with rice and garlic chives to make a tasty accompaniment to vegetarian dishes, fish or chicken.

SERVES 4

1 small onion, finely chopped
2 green chillies, seeded and
    finely chopped
60ml/4 tbsp groundnut (peanut) oil
25g/1oz garlic chives, chopped
15g/¹/₂oz fresh coriander (cilantro)
600ml/1 pint/2¹/₂ cups vegetable or
    mushroom stock
350g/12oz/generous 1³/₄ cups long grain
    rice, washed and drained
2.5ml/¹/₂ tsp sea salt
250g/9oz mixed mushrooms,
    thickly sliced
50g/2oz cashew nuts, fried in 15ml/
    1 tbsp olive oil until golden brown
plenty of ground black pepper

1 In a pan, gently cook the onion and chillies in half the oil, stirring, for 10–12 minutes. Set half the garlic chives aside. Cut the stalks off the coriander and set the leaves aside. Purée the remaining chives and the coriander stalks with the stock in a food processor.

2 Gently fry the rice and onions, stirring often, for 4–5 minutes. Add the stock, salt and black pepper. Bring to the boil, stir and reduce the heat to very low. Cover with a lid and cook for 15–20 minutes until the rice absorbs all the liquid.

3 Remove from the heat. Lay a folded dish towel over the pan, under the lid. Press the lid to wedge it in place. Leave for a further 10 minutes.

4 Cook the mushrooms in the remaining oil for 5–6 minutes until tender and browned. Add the remaining garlic chives and cook for another 1–2 minutes. Stir the cooked mushroom and chive mixture and chopped coriander leaves into the rice. Season to taste, then transfer to a warmed serving dish and serve immediately, scattered with the fried cashew nuts.

Nutritional information per portion: Energy 504kcal/2100kJ; Protein 10.4g; Carbohydrate 73.8g, of which sugars 1.8g; Fat 18.2g, of which saturates 2.6g; Cholesterol 0mg; Calcium 41mg; Fibre 1.6g; Sodium 533mg.

Orange candied sweet potatoes

Organic sweet potatoes are free of the fungicides sprayed on non-organic tubers and are an excellent source of vitamins, including cancer-preventing betacarotene.

SERVES 8

900g/2lb sweet potatoes
250ml/8fl oz/1 cup orange juice
50ml/2fl oz/¹/₄ cup maple syrup
5ml/1 tsp freshly grated root ginger
7.5ml/1¹/₂ tsp ground cinnamon
6.5ml/1¹/₄ tsp ground cardamom
2.5ml/¹/₂ tsp salt
ground black pepper
ground cinnamon and orange segments,
**   to garnish**

1 Preheat the oven to 180°C/350°F/Gas 4. Peel and dice the potatoes and then steam them for 5 minutes.

2 Meanwhile, stir the remaining ingredients together. Spread out on to a non-stick shallow baking tin (pan).

3 Scatter the potatoes over the baking tin. Cook for 1 hour, stirring every 15 minutes, until they are tender and well coated in the spicy syrup.

4 Serve garnished with orange segments and ground cinnamon.

COOK'S TIP
This popular American dish is traditionally served with roast turkey at Thanksgiving and Christmas. Serve with extra orange segments to make it really special.

Nutritional information per portion: Energy 40kcal/169kJ; Protein 0.3g; Carbohydrate 10.1g, of which sugars 8.3g; Fat 0.1g, of which saturates 0g; Cholesterol 0mg; Calcium 7mg; Fibre 0.3g; Sodium 148mg.

Florets Polonaise

Simple steamed organic vegetables become something very special with this pretty egg topping. They make a perfect dinner party side dish or are great with a weekday supper.

SERVES 6

500g/1¼lb mixed vegetables, such as
    cauliflower, broccoli, romanesco
    and calabrese
50g/2oz/¼ cup butter or 60ml/4 tbsp
    extra virgin olive oil
finely grated rind of ½ lemon
1 large garlic clove, crushed
25g/1oz/½ cup fresh breadcrumbs,
    lightly baked or grilled (broiled)
    until crisp
2 eggs, hard-boiled
sea salt and ground black pepper

1 Trim the vegetables and break into equal-size florets. Place the florets in a steamer over a pan of boiling water and steam for 5–7 minutes, until just tender.

2 Toss the steamed vegetables in butter or oil and transfer to a serving dish.

3 While the vegetables are cooking, thoroughly mix together the lemon rind, garlic, seasoning and baked or grilled breadcrumbs. Then, finely chop the eggs and mix together with the remaining ingredients. Sprinkle the chopped egg mixture over the cooked vegetables and then serve immediately.

Nutritional information per portion: Energy 71kcal/297kJ; Protein 5.2g; Carbohydrate 4.7g, of which sugars 1.4g; Fat 3.6g, of which saturates 0.7g; Cholesterol 32mg; Calcium 57mg; Fibre 2.3g; Sodium 50mg.

Roasted shallot and squash salad

This is especially good served with a grain or starchy salad, based on rice or couscous, for example. Serve with plenty of home-made organic bread to mop up the juices.

SERVES 4–6

75ml/5 tbsp olive oil

15ml/1 tbsp balsamic vinegar, plus a little extra, if you like

15ml/1 tbsp sweet soy sauce

350g/12oz shallots, peeled but left whole

3 fresh red chillies

1 butternut squash, peeled, seeded and cut into chunks

5ml/1 tsp finely chopped fresh thyme

15g/¹/₂oz flat leaf parsley

1 small garlic clove, finely chopped

75g/3oz/³/₄ cup walnuts, chopped

150g/5oz feta cheese

sea salt and ground black pepper

1 Heat the oven to 200°C/400°F/ Gas 6. Beat the olive oil, balsamic vinegar and soy sauce in a large bowl. Season with a little salt and lots of freshly ground black pepper.

2 Toss the shallots and two chillies in the oil mixture, then roast in a large roasting pan or ovenproof dish for 15 minutes, stirring once or twice.

3 Add the butternut squash chunks and roast for a further 30–35 minutes, stirring once, until the squash is tender and browned.

4 Remove from the oven, stir in the chopped thyme and leave to cool.

5 Chop together the parsley and garlic, and mix with the walnuts. Seed and finely chop the remaining chilli.

6 Stir the parsley, garlic and walnut mixture into the vegetables. Add chopped chilli to taste and adjust the seasoning, adding a little extra balsamic vinegar, if you like. Crumble the feta and add to the salad. Transfer to a serving dish and serve immediately.

Nutritional information per portion: Energy 275kcal/1136kJ; Protein 7.7g; Carbohydrate 9.3g, of which sugars 7g; Fat 23.2g, of which saturates 5.6g; Cholesterol 18mg; Calcium 165mg; Fibre 2.9g; Sodium 541mg.

Tofu and vegetable Thai curry

Non-organic soya products, including tofu, are often made from genetically modified beans that are resistant to pesticides. By using organic tofu in this fragrant curry, you benefit from its great texture and superior nutritional value while helping to protect the Earth.

SERVES 4

175g/6oz tofu, drained
45ml/3 tbsp dark soy sauce
15ml/1 tbsp sesame oil
5ml/1 tsp chilli sauce
2.5cm/1in piece fresh root ginger,
   finely grated
225g/8oz cauliflower
225g/8oz broccoli
30ml/2 tbsp sunflower oil
1 onion, sliced
400ml/14fl oz/1²/₃ cups coconut milk
150ml/¹/₄ pint/²/₃ cup water
1 red (bell) pepper, seeded and chopped
175g/6oz green beans, halved

115g/4oz/1¹/₂ cups shiitake or button
   (white) mushrooms, halved
shredded spring onions (scallions), to garnish
boiled brown rice or noodles, to serve

FOR THE CURRY PASTE

2 chillies, seeded and chopped
1 lemon grass stalk, chopped
2.5cm/1in piece fresh galangal or fresh root
   ginger, chopped
2 kaffir lime leaves
10ml/2 tsp ground coriander
a few sprigs fresh coriander (cilantro),
   including the stalks

1 Cut the drained tofu into 2.5cm/1in cubes and place in an ovenproof dish. Mix together the soy sauce, sesame oil, chilli sauce and ginger, and pour over the tofu. Toss gently to coat all the cubes evenly, then leave to marinate for at least 2 hours or overnight if possible, turning and basting the tofu occasionally.

2 To make the curry paste, place the chopped chillies, lemon grass, galangal, kaffir lime leaves, ground coriander and fresh coriander in a food processor, and process for a few seconds until well blended. Add 45ml/3 tbsp water and process to a thick paste.

3 Preheat the oven to 190°C/375°F/Gas 5. Using a large sharp knife, cut the cauliflower and broccoli into small florets and cut any stalks into thin slices.

4 Heat the sunflower oil in a frying pan, add the sliced onion and gently fry for about 8 minutes, or until soft and lightly browned. Stir in the prepared curry paste and the coconut milk.

5 Add the water and bring to the boil, then stir in the red pepper, green beans, cauliflower and broccoli. Transfer to an earthenware casserole or Chinese sand pot. Cover and place in the oven.

6 Stir the tofu and marinade, then place the dish in the top of the oven and cook for 30 minutes. After 30 minutes, stir the tofu and marinade into the curry with the mushrooms.

7 Reduce the oven temperature to 180°C/350°F/Gas 4 and cook for about 15 minutes more, or until the vegetables are tender. Garnish with spring onions and serve with boiled rice or noodles.

Nutritional information per portion: Energy 169kcal/707kJ; Protein 11g; Carbohydrate 13.7g, of which sugars 12.3g; Fat 8.2g, of which saturates 1.4g; Cholesterol 0mg; Calcium 356mg; Fibre 5.4g; Sodium 932mg.

Spaghetti with eggs and bacon

Organic ingredients really enhance the flavours of simple, classic dishes such as this Italian favourite, which makes a great last-minute supper.

SERVES 4

30ml/2 tbsp olive oil
1 small onion, finely chopped
1 large garlic clove, crushed
8 pancetta or rindless smoked streaky (fatty) bacon rashers (strips), cut into 1cm/½in strips
350g/12oz fresh or dried spaghetti
4 eggs
90–120ml/6–8 tbsp reduced-fat crème fraîche
60ml/4 tbsp freshly grated Parmesan cheese or premium Italian-style vegetarian cheese, plus extra to serve
sea salt and ground black pepper

1 In a large pan, gently fry the onion and garlic in the oil for 5 minutes until softened. Add the pancetta or bacon and cook for 10 minutes, stirring.

2 Meanwhile, cook the spaghetti in a large pan of salted boiling water for 10 minutes, or according to the instructions on the packet, until *al dente*.

3 Put the eggs, crème fraîche and grated Parmesan in a bowl. Stir in plenty of black pepper, then beat together well.

4 Drain the pasta thoroughly, tip it into the pan with the pancetta or bacon and toss well to mix.

5 Turn off the heat under the pan, then immediately add the egg mixture and toss thoroughly so that it cooks lightly and coats the pasta.

6 Season to taste, then divide the spaghetti among four warmed bowls and sprinkle with freshly ground black pepper. Serve with extra grated cheese.

Nutritional information per portion: Energy 708kcal/2966kJ; Protein 30.7g; Carbohydrate 66.6g, of which sugars 4.2g; Fat 37.5g, of which saturates 15.5g; Cholesterol 261mg; Calcium 250mg; Fibre 2.8g; Sodium 824mg.

Potato-topped fish pie

This traditional Scottish dish should be prepared from wild fish such as hoki or other white fish caught sustainably. Always ensure you buy wild fish bearing the MSC logo.

SERVES 4

675g/1½lb hoki fillets (or alternative)
300ml/½ pint/1¼ cups milk/soya milk
½ lemon, sliced
1 bay leaf
1 fresh thyme sprig
4–5 black peppercorns
50g/2oz/¼ cup butter or
  non-hydrogenated margarine
25g/1oz/¼ cup plain (all-purpose) flour
30ml/2 tbsp chopped fresh parsley
5ml/1 tsp anchovy essence (paste)
150g/5oz/2 cups shiitake or chestnut
  mushrooms, sliced
sea salt, ground black pepper and
  cayenne pepper
450g/1lb potatoes, cooked and mashed
  with milk or soya milk
50g/2oz/¼ cup butter or
  non-hydrogenated margarine
2 tomatoes, sliced
25g/1oz/¼ cup grated Cheddar cheese

1 Put the fish skin side down in a shallow pan. Add the milk, lemon slices, bay leaf, thyme and peppercorns. Bring to the boil, then lower the heat and poach gently for 5 minutes until just cooked. Strain off and reserve the milk. Remove the fish skin and flake the flesh, discarding any bones.

2 In a small pan, gently cook half the butter and flour for 1 minute. Add the reserved milk and boil, whisking, until smooth and creamy. Stir in the parsley and anchovy essence and season to taste.

3 Heat the remaining butter in a frying pan, add the sliced mushrooms and sauté until tender. Season and add to the flaked fish. Mix the sauce into the fish and stir gently to combine. Transfer the mixture to an ovenproof casserole.

4 Heat the oven to 200°C/400°F/Gas 6. Beat the mashed potato with butter until creamy. Season, then spread over the fish. Fork the surface and arrange the tomato around the edge. Sprinkle the exposed topping with grated cheese. Bake for 20–25 minutes until the topping is browned. If you prefer, finish the browning under a hot grill (broiler).

Nutritional information per portion: Energy 458kcal/1921kJ; Protein 29.5g; Carbohydrate 32.8g, of which sugars 5.8g; Fat 25g, of which saturates 3.7g; Cholesterol 74mg; Calcium 216mg; Fibre 1g; Sodium 867mg.

Grilled mackerel with spicy dhal

Oily fish such as mackerel are great for the nervous system. They are also well complemented by a tart or sour accompaniment, like these delicious tamarind-flavoured lentils or split peas.

SERVES 4

250g/9oz/generous 1 cup red lentils, or
    yellow split peas (soaked overnight)
1 litre/1³/₄ pints/4 cups water
30ml/2 tbsp sunflower oil
2.5ml/¹/₂ tsp each mustard seeds, cumin
    seeds, fennel seeds and fenugreek or
    cardamom seeds
5ml/1 tsp ground turmeric
3–4 dried red chillies, crumbled
30ml/2 tbsp tamarind paste
30ml/2 tbsp chopped fresh
    coriander (cilantro)
4 mackerels
ground black pepper
fresh red chilli slices and finely chopped
    coriander, to garnish
flat bread and tomatoes, to serve

1 Rinse the lentils or split peas, drain them thoroughly and put them in a pan. Pour in the water and bring to the boil. Lower the heat, partially cover the pan and simmer the lentils or split peas for 30–40 minutes, stirring occasionally, until they are tender and mushy.

2 Heat the oil in a wok or shallow pan. Add the mustard seeds, then cover and cook for a few seconds until they pop. Remove the lid, add the rest of the seeds, with the turmeric and chillies, and fry for a few more seconds.

3 Stir in the lentils or split peas and the tamarind paste and mix well. Bring to the boil, then simmer for 10 minutes until thick. Stir in the coriander.

4 Clean the fish, then heat a ridged griddle or the grill (broiler) until very hot. Make six diagonal slashes on either side of each fish and remove the head. Season, then grill (broil) for 5–7 minutes on each side. Serve, garnished with red chilli and chopped coriander, accompanied by the dhal, flat bread and tomatoes.

Nutritional information per portion: Energy 586kcal/2453kJ; Protein 43.3g; Carbohydrate 36.5g, of which sugars 2.8g; Fat 30.6g, of which saturates 5.7g; Cholesterol 81mg; Calcium 72mg; Fibre 3.6g; Sodium 121mg.

Salmon and rice gratin

This all-in-one supper dish is ideal for informal autumn entertaining as it can be made in advance and reheated for about half an hour before being served with a tossed salad.

SERVES 6

675g/1¹/₂lb fresh salmon fillet, skinned
1 bay leaf
a few parsley stalks
1 litre/1³/₄ pints/4 cups water
400g/14oz/2 cups basmati rice, soaked
    and drained
30–45ml/2–3 tbsp chopped fresh parsley,
    plus extra to garnish
175g/6oz/1¹/₂ cups grated
    Cheddar cheese
3 hard-boiled eggs, chopped
sea salt and ground black pepper

FOR THE SAUCE

1 litre/1³/₄ pints/4 cups milk or soya milk
40g/1¹/₂oz/¹/₃ cup plain
    (all-purpose) flour
40g/1¹/₂oz/3 tbsp butter or
    non-hydrogenated margarine
5ml/1 tsp mild curry paste

1 In a wide, shallow pan, poach the fish, with the bay leaf and parsley stalks, a little salt, plenty of black pepper, and water, for 12 minutes until tender. Lift out with a slotted spoon. Strain the cooking liquid into a large pan. Leave to cool. Remove any visible bones and flake gently into bitesize pieces with a fork.

2 Add the rice to the pan with the fish-poaching liquid. Bring to the boil, lower the heat, cover with a lid and simmer for 10 minutes, without lifting the lid. Remove from the heat and, without lifting the lid, leave for 5 minutes.

3 To make the sauce, bring the milk, flour and butter or margarine to the boil over a low heat in a pan, whisking constantly until smooth and thick. Stir in the curry paste with salt and pepper to taste. Simmer for 2 minutes.

4 Heat the grill (broiler). Remove the sauce from the heat and stir in the parsley, rice and half the cheese. With a metal spoon, fold in the flaked fish and eggs. Spoon into a shallow gratin dish and sprinkle with the remaining cheese. Grill until the topping is golden and bubbling. Garnish and serve.

Nutritional information per portion: Energy 752kcal/3137kJ; Protein 44.8g; Carbohydrate 66.5g, of which sugars 8.2g; Fat 33.5g, of which saturates 14.5g; Cholesterol 204mg; Calcium 492mg; Fibre 0.6g; Sodium 411mg.

Sole with wild mushrooms

If possible, use organic chanterelles for this dish; their glowing orange colour goes wonderfully with the golden sauce. Otherwise, use any other pale-coloured or oyster mushrooms.

SERVES 4

4 Dover sole fillets, about 115g/4oz
   each, skinned
50g/2oz/¼ cup butter or
   non-hydrogenated margarine
500ml/17fl oz/generous 2 cups fish stock
150g/5oz/2 cups chanterelles or oyster
   mushrooms, cleaned and wiped
a large pinch of saffron threads
150ml/¼ pint/⅔ cup double (heavy)
   cream or soya cream
1 egg yolk
sea salt and ground white pepper
flat leaf parsley sprigs, to garnish
boiled new potatoes and steamed
   broccoli florets, to serve

1 Heat the oven to 200°C/400°F/Gas 6. Cut the fillets in half lengthways and place on a board with the skinned side uppermost. Season, then roll them up. With a little butter, grease a baking dish large enough to hold the fillets in a single layer. Arrange the rolls in it, then pour over the fish stock. Cover tightly with foil and bake for 12–15 minutes until cooked through.

2 In a frying pan, sauté the mushrooms (halve the large ones) in the remaining butter for 3–4 minutes. Season with salt and pepper and keep hot. Lift the fillets out of the dish and place on a heated serving dish. Keep hot. Strain the liquid into a small pan. Add the saffron and reduce to 250ml/8fl oz/1 cup over a high heat. Stir in the cream and let the sauce bubble for a moment.

3 Lightly beat the egg yolk in a small bowl, pour on a little of the hot sauce and stir well. Stir the mixture into the remaining sauce in the pan and cook very gently for 1–2 minutes until slightly thickened. Season to taste. Stir in the chanterelles and pour the sauce over the sole fillets. Garnish with parsley and serve.

Nutritional information per portion: Energy 411kcal/1699kJ; Protein 24.7g; Carbohydrate 0.9g, of which sugars 0.8g; Fat 34.2g, of which saturates 19.5g; Cholesterol 191mg; Calcium 65mg; Fibre 0.4g; Sodium 213mg.

Chicken with cashew nuts

This popular Chinese dish is quick and easy to make and can be enjoyed to the full by using good-quality organic products that are full of flavour.

SERVES 4

350g/12oz skinless chicken breast fillets
pinch of ground white pepper
15ml/1 tbsp dry sherry
300ml/1/2 pint/11/4 cups chicken stock
15ml/1 tbsp sunflower oil
1 garlic clove, finely chopped
1 small carrot, cut into cubes
1/2 cucumber, about 75g/3oz, cut into
   1cm/1/2in cubes
50g/2oz/1/2 cup drained canned
   bamboo shoots, cut into 1cm/1/2in
   cubes (optional)
5ml/1 tsp cornflour (cornstarch)
15ml/1 tbsp soy sauce
25g/1oz/1/4 cup dry-roasted cashew nuts
2.5ml/1/2 tsp sesame oil
noodles, to serve

1 Cut the chicken into 2cm/3/4in cubes. Place the cubes in a bowl, stir in the white pepper and sherry, cover and marinate for 15 minutes.

2 Bring the stock to the boil in a large pan. Add the chicken and cook, stirring, for 3 minutes. Drain, reserving 90ml/6 tbsp of the stock, and set aside.

3 Heat the sunflower oil in a large non-stick frying pan until it is very hot, add the finely chopped garlic and stir-fry for a few seconds. Add the cubed carrot, cucumber and bamboo shoots, if using, and continue to stir-fry the vegetables over a medium heat for 2 minutes.

4 Stir in the chicken and reserved stock. Mix the cornflour with the soy sauce and add the mixture to the pan. Cook, stirring, until the sauce thickens slightly. Finally, add the cashew nuts and sesame oil. Toss to mix thoroughly, then serve with noodles.

Nutritional information per portion: Energy 153kcal/645kJ; Protein 22.9g; Carbohydrate 5.1g, of which sugars 2.8g; Fat 4.3g, of which saturates 0.9g; Cholesterol 61mg; Calcium 14mg; Fibre 0.7g; Sodium 342mg.

Duck sausages with spicy plum sauce

A variety of organic sausages is available direct from farmers and small butchers, and any pork or game sausages would work in this dish. Rich duck sausages are best baked in their own juices.

SERVES 4

8–12 duck sausages

FOR THE SWEET POTATO MASH

1.5kg/3¹/₄lb sweet potatoes, cut into chunks
25g/1oz/2 tbsp butter or 30ml/2 tbsp olive oil
60ml/4 tbsp milk
sea salt and ground black pepper

FOR THE PLUM SAUCE

30ml/2 tbsp olive oil
1 small onion, chopped
1 small red chilli, seeded and chopped
450g/1lb plums, stoned and chopped
30ml/2 tbsp red wine vinegar
45ml/3 tbsp clear honey

1 Heat the oven to 190°C/375°F/ Gas 5. Arrange the duck sausages in a single layer in a large, shallow ovenproof dish. Bake the sausages, uncovered, in the oven for 25–30 minutes, turning the sausages two or three times during cooking, to ensure that they brown and cook evenly.

2 Meanwhile, put the sweet potatoes in a pan and add water to cover. Bring to the boil, then reduce the heat and simmer for 20 minutes, or until tender.

3 Drain and mash the potatoes, then place the pan over a low heat. Stir frequently for 5 minutes to dry out the mashed potato. Beat in the butter or oil and milk, and season to taste.

4 Make the plum sauce. Heat the oil in a small pan and fry the onion and chilli gently for 5 minutes. Stir in the plums, vinegar and honey, then simmer gently for 10 minutes.

5 Serve the sausages with the sweet potato mash and plum sauce.

Nutritional information per portion: Energy 894kcal/3755kJ; Protein 17.8g; Carbohydrate 110.8g, of which sugars 42.9g; Fat 45.5g, of which saturates 17.9g; Cholesterol 67mg; Calcium 170mg; Fibre 11.6g; Sodium 1052mg.

Spicy venison casserole

Being high in flavour but low in saturated fat, organic venison is a good choice for healthy, yet rich, casseroles. Cranberries and orange bring a delicious fruitiness to this spicy recipe.

SERVES 4

15ml/1 tbsp olive oil
1 onion, chopped
2 celery sticks, sliced
10ml/2 tsp ground allspice
15ml/1 tbsp plain (all-purpose) or
    wholemeal (whole-wheat) flour
675g/1¹/₂lb stewing venison, cubed
225g/8oz fresh or frozen cranberries
grated rind and juice of 1 orange
900ml/1¹/₂ pints/3³/₄ cups beef or
    venison stock
sea salt and ground black pepper

1 Heat the oil in a flameproof casserole. Add the onion and celery. Fry for 5 minutes, or until softened.

2 Mix the ground allspice with the flour and either spread the mixture out on a large plate or place in a large plastic bag. Toss a few pieces of venison at a time in the flour mixture until all are lightly coated. Spread the floured venison out on a large plate until ready to cook.

3 When the onion and celery are just softened, remove them from the casserole using a slotted spoon and set aside.

4 Add the venison pieces to the casserole in batches. Cook until well browned and sealed on all sides.

5 Add the cranberries and the orange rind and juice to the casserole along with the stock and stir well. Return the vegetables and the browned venison to the casserole and heat until simmering. Cover tightly and reduce the heat.

6 Simmer for 45 minutes, or until the venison is tender, stirring occasionally. Season the casserole to taste with a little salt and plenty of ground black pepper before serving.

Nutritional information per portion: Energy 242kcal/1025kJ; Protein 38.3g; Carbohydrate 10.4g, of which sugars 7.2g; Fat 6.6g, of which saturates 1.8g; Cholesterol 84mg; Calcium 27mg; Fibre 1.4g; Sodium 105mg.

Stuffed roast loin of pork with apple sauce

The secret of a good roast with apple sauce is simple, good-quality ingredients, such as organic pork and traditionally made cider.

SERVES 6

15ml/1 tbsp light olive oil
2 leeks, chopped
150g/5oz/²/₃ cup ready-to-eat dried
    apricots, chopped
150g/5oz/scant 1 cup dried dates, stoned
    and chopped
75g/3oz/1¹/₂ cups fresh white or wholemeal
    (whole-wheat) breadcrumbs

2 eggs, beaten
15ml/1 tbsp fresh thyme leaves
1.5kg/3¹/₄lb boned loin of pork
sea salt and ground black pepper

FOR THE APPLE SAUCE
450g/1lb cooking apples
30ml/2 tbsp cider or water
25g/1oz/2 tbsp butter or 30ml/2 tbsp olive oil

1 Preheat the oven to 220°C/425°F/Gas 7. Heat the oil in a large pan and cook the leeks until softened. Stir in the apricots, dates, breadcrumbs, eggs and thyme, and season with salt and pepper.

2 Lay the pork skin side up, and use a sharp knife to score the rind crossways.

3 Turn the meat over and cut down the centre of the joint to within 1cm/¹/₂in of the rind and fat, then work from the middle outwards towards one side, cutting most of the meat off the rind but keeping a 1cm/¹/₂in layer of meat on top of the rind. Cut to within 2.5cm/1in of the side of the joint. Repeat on the other side of the joint.

4 Spoon half the stuffing over the joint, then fold the meat over it. Tie the joint back into its original shape, then place in a roasting pan and rub the skin with salt. Roast the pork for 40 minutes, then reduce the oven temperature to 190°C/375°F/Gas 5 and cook for a further 1¹/₂ hours, or until the meat is tender and cooked through.

5 Meanwhile, shape the remaining stuffing into walnut-size balls. Arrange on a tray, cover with clear film (plastic wrap) and chill until 20 minutes before the pork is cooked. Then add the stuffing balls to the roasting pan and baste them with the cooking juices from the meat.

6 When cooked, cover the meat closely with foil and leave to stand in a warm place for 10 minutes before carving.

7 To make the apple sauce, peel, core and chop the apples, then place in a small pan with the cider or water and cook for 5–10 minutes, stirring occasionally, or until very soft. Beat well or process in a food processor or blender to make smooth apple sauce. Beat in the butter or oil. Reheat the apple sauce just before serving, if necessary.

8 Carve the joint into thick slices. If the crackling is very hard, you may find that it is easier to slice the crackling off the joint first, before carving the meat, then cut the crackling into serving pieces using poultry shears or a heavy, sharp chef's knife or cleaver. Serve the stuffed loin of pork with the crackling, stuffing balls, apple sauce and a selection of seasonal autumn vegetables.

Nutritional information per portion: Energy 398kcal/1667kJ; Protein 49.7g; Carbohydrate 13g, of which sugars 8.2g; Fat 15.5g, of which saturates 7.1g; Cholesterol 160mg; Calcium 50mg; Fibre 0.7g; Sodium 239mg.

Moussaka

In this traditional eastern Mediterranean dish, layers of minced organic mutton, aubergines, tomatoes and onions are topped with a creamy yogurt and cheese sauce.

SERVES 4

450g/1lb aubergines (eggplant)
150ml/^{1}/$_{4}$ pint/^{2}/$_{3}$ cup olive oil
1 large onion, chopped
2–3 garlic cloves, finely chopped
675g/1^{1}/$_{2}$lb lean minced (ground) mutton
15ml/1 tbsp plain (all-purpose) flour
400g/14oz can chopped tomatoes
30ml/2 tbsp chopped mixed herbs such as
   parsley, marjoram and oregano
sea salt and ground black pepper

FOR THE TOPPING

300ml/^{1}/$_{2}$ pint/1^{1}/$_{4}$ cups natural
   (plain) yogurt
2 eggs
25g/1oz feta cheese, crumbled
25g/1oz/^{1}/$_{3}$ cup freshly grated Parmesan
   cheese or premium Italian-style
   vegetarian cheese

1 Slice the aubergines and layer them in a colander. Sprinkle with salt and cover with a plate and a weight, then leave to drain for about 30 minutes. Drain the aubergines, rinse well and pat dry with kitchen paper.

2 Heat 45ml/3 tbsp of oil in a large, heavy pan. Fry the onion and garlic until softened, but not coloured. Add the mutton and cook over a high heat, stirring, until browned. Stir in the flour, then the tomatoes, herbs and seasoning. Bring to the boil, reduce the heat and simmer for 20 minutes.

3 Heat a little olive oil in a large frying pan. Add some aubergine slices in a single layer. Cook until golden on both sides, then remove from the pan. Repeat in batches.

4 Heat the oven to 180°C/350°F/Gas 4. Arrange half the slices in a large, shallow ovenproof dish. Top with half the meat and tomato mixture. Add the remaining slices and top with the remaining mixture.

5 To make the topping, beat together the yogurt and eggs, then mix in the feta and Parmesan or Italian-style cheeses. Pour the mixture over the meat and spread it evenly. Transfer the moussaka to the oven and bake for 35–40 minutes, or until golden and bubbling.

Nutritional information per portion: Energy 588kcal/2445kJ; Protein 37.9g; Carbohydrate 14.8g, of which sugars 3.7g; Fat 40.9g, of which saturates 18.2g; Cholesterol 206mg; Calcium 379mg; Fibre 2.4g; Sodium 506mg.

Honey-baked figs with hazelnut ice cream

Organic figs have a deliciously intense flavour. They are smaller than non-organic fruit as they are not forced to absorb water during growing, so you may need three per person.

SERVES 4

1 lemon grass stalk, finely chopped
1 cinnamon stick, roughly broken
60ml/4 tbsp clear honey
200ml/7fl oz/scant 1 cup water
8 large or 12 small figs

FOR THE HAZELNUT ICE CREAM
450ml/³/₄ pint/scant 2 cups double (heavy)
   cream or soya cream
50g/2oz/¹/₄ cup unrefined caster (superfine)
   sugar or rapadura
3 egg yolks
1.5ml/¹/₄ tsp vanilla extract
75g/3oz/³/₄ cup hazelnuts

1 To make the ice cream, place the cream in a pan and heat slowly until it is almost boiling. Place the sugar and egg yolks in a bowl and whisk until thick and creamy.

2 Pour a little cream on to the egg yolk mixture and stir. Pour into the pan and mix with the rest of the cream. Cook over a low heat, stirring constantly, until the mixture lightly coats the back of the spoon – do not allow it to boil. Pour into a bowl, stir in the vanilla extract and leave to cool.

3 Preheat the oven to 180°C/350°F/Gas 4. Place the hazelnuts on a baking sheet and roast for 10–12 minutes, or until they are golden brown. Leave the nuts to cool, then place them in a food processor or blender and process until they are coarsely ground.

4 Transfer the ice cream mixture to a metal or plastic freezer container and freeze for 2 hours, or until the mixture feels firm around the edge. Remove the container from the freezer and whisk the ice cream to break down the ice crystals. Stir in the ground hazelnuts and freeze the mixture again until half-frozen. Whisk again, then freeze until firm.

5 Place the lemon grass, cinnamon stick, honey and water in a small pan and heat slowly until boiling. Simmer the mixture for 5 minutes, then leave the syrup to stand for 15 minutes.

6 Preheat the oven to 200°C/400°F/Gas 6. Meanwhile, carefully cut the figs into quarters, leaving them intact at the bases. Place the figs in an ovenproof baking dish and pour over the honey-flavoured syrup.

7 Cover the dish tightly with foil and bake the figs for about 15 minutes, or until tender.

8 Take the ice cream from the freezer about 10 minutes before serving, to soften slightly. Transfer the figs to serving plates. Strain a little of the cooking liquid over the figs and then serve them with a scoop or two of hazelnut ice cream.

Nutritional information per portion: Energy 433kcal/1816kJ; Protein 7.8g; Carbohydrate 53.6g, of which sugars 52.1g; Fat 21.2g, of which saturates 7g; Cholesterol 24mg; Calcium 227mg; Fibre 4.2g; Sodium 88mg.

Sticky pear pudding

Pears are at their best in autumn and, combined with other organic ingredients such as cloves, coffee and maple syrup, they form the basis of this indulgent dessert.

SERVES 6

30ml/2 tbsp ground coffee
15ml/1 tbsp near-boiling water
4 ripe pears
juice of 1/2 orange
50g/2oz/1/2 cup toasted hazelnuts
115g/4oz/1/2 cup butter or non-
   hydrogenated margarine, softened
115g/4oz/generous 1/2 cup unrefined caster
   (superfine) sugar or rapadura, plus an
   extra 15ml/1 tbsp for baking
2 eggs, beaten

50g/2oz/1/2 cup self-raising (self-rising)
   flour, sifted
pinch of ground cloves
8 whole cloves (optional)
45ml/3 tbsp maple syrup
fine strips of orange rind, to decorate

FOR THE ORANGE CREAM
300ml/1/2 pint/11/4 cups whipping cream
15ml/1 tbsp unrefined icing (confectioners')
   sugar, sifted
finely grated rind of 1/2 orange

1 Heat the oven to 180°C/350°F/Gas 4. Grease a 20cm/8in loose-based sandwich tin (layer cake pan). In a bowl, infuse the coffee in the water for 4 minutes, then strain through a fine sieve (strainer).

2 Peel, halve and core the pears, then thinly slice across each half part of the way through. Brush with orange juice. Finely grind the hazelnuts in a coffee grinder. Beat the butter and caster sugar together until very light and fluffy. Gradually beat in the eggs, then fold in the flour, ground cloves, hazelnuts and coffee. Spoon into the sandwich tin and level the surface with a spatula.

3 Dry the pears on kitchen paper and arrange in the sponge mixture, flat side down. Lightly press two whole cloves, if using, into each half. Brush with 15ml/ 1 tbsp maple syrup and sprinkle over 15ml/1 tbsp caster sugar. Bake for 45–50 minutes, or until firm and well risen.

4 Whip the cream, icing sugar and orange rind into soft peaks. Spoon into a serving dish and chill. Allow the sponge to cool for about 10 minutes in the tin, then remove and place on a serving plate. Brush with maple syrup, decorate with orange rind and serve warm with the orange cream.

Nutritional information per portion: Energy 580kcal/2410kJ; Protein 5.6g; Carbohydrate 44.8g, of which sugars 38.3g; Fat 43.3g, of which saturates 23.5g; Cholesterol 157mg; Calcium 88mg; Fibre 3g; Sodium 178mg.

Custard tart with plums

When this tart is made with really ripe, organic sweet plums, it makes a wonderful hot or cold weekend dessert. Serve it with thick cream, ice cream or Greek yogurt.

SERVES 4–6

175g/6oz/1¹/₂ cups plain (all-purpose)
   flour, sifted
pinch of salt
45ml/3 tbsp unrefined caster (superfine)
   sugar or rapadura
115g/4oz/¹/₂ cup unsalted (sweet)
   butter or non-hydrogenated margarine
2 eggs, plus 2 egg yolks
350g/12oz ripe plums
300ml/¹/₂ pint/1¹/₄ cups milk or
   soya milk
few drops of vanilla extract
toasted flaked (sliced) almonds and
   sifted unrefined icing (confectioners')
   sugar, to decorate

1 Combine the flour, salt, 15ml/1 tbsp of the sugar, the butter and one egg in a food processor. Tip the mixture on to a clean, lightly floured surface and bring together in a ball. Wrap in clear film (plastic wrap) and chill for 10 minutes.

2 Flour a deep 18cm/7in square or 20cm/8in round loose-bottomed flan tin (pan). Roll out the pastry to line the tin. Chill for another 10–20 minutes.

3 Heat the oven to 200°C/400°F/Gas 6. Line the pastry case with baking parchment, fill with baking beans and bake for 15 minutes. Remove the paper and beans, reduce to 180°C/350°F/Gas 4 and bake for 5–10 minutes until dry.

4 Halve and stone the plums, and arrange in the pastry case. Whisk together the remaining egg and yolks, sugar, milk and vanilla extract and pour over the fruit.

5 Return the tart to the oven and bake for 25–30 minutes, or until the custard is just firm to the touch. Remove from the oven and allow to cool. Sprinkle with flaked almonds and dredge with icing sugar before serving.

Nutritional information per portion: Energy 396kcal/1652kJ; Protein 5.5g; Carbohydrate 37.2g, of which sugars 18.2g; Fat 25.2g, of which saturates 14.7g; Cholesterol 155mg; Calcium 74mg; Fibre 1.7g; Sodium 104mg.

Hot blackberry and apple soufflés

The deliciously tart autumn flavours of blackberry and apple complement each other perfectly to make a light, mouthwatering hot pudding.

MAKES 6

butter or non-hydrogenated margarine,
    for greasing
150g/5oz/³/₄ cup unrefined caster
    (superfine) sugar or rapadura, plus
    extra for dusting
350g/12oz/3 cups blackberries
1 large cooking apple, peeled and
    finely diced
grated rind and juice of 1 orange
3 egg whites
unrefined icing (confectioners') sugar,
    for dusting

1 Heat the oven to 200°C/400°F/Gas 6. Generously grease six 150ml/ ¹/₄ pint/²/₃ cup soufflé dishes with butter and dust with caster sugar.

2 Heat a baking sheet in the oven. Cook the blackberries, apple, orange rind and juice in a pan for 10 minutes or until the apple has pulped down well. Strain into a bowl. Stir in 50g/2oz/¹/₄ cup of caster sugar. Leave to cool.

3 Put a spoonful of the fruit purée into each soufflé dish and spread evenly. Set the dishes aside.

4 In a grease-free bowl, whisk the egg whites into stiff peaks. Gradually whisk in the remaining caster sugar to make a stiff, glossy meringue mixture. Fold in the remaining fruit purée and spoon the flavoured meringue into the dishes. Level the tops with a metal spatula and run a table knife around the edge of each dish.

5 Place the dishes on the hot baking sheet and bake for 10–15 minutes until the soufflés are well risen and lightly browned. Dust with icing sugar and serve.

Nutritional information per portion: Energy 123kcal/522kJ; Protein 2.1g; Carbohydrate 30.1g, of which sugars 30.1g; Fat 0.1g, of which saturates 0g; Cholesterol 0mg; Calcium 38mg; Fibre 2g; Sodium 33mg.

Plum charlottes with foamy Calvados sauce

A variety of different types of delicious organic plums are available at this time of year – from tangy yellow greengages to sweet and juicy Victorias.

SERVES 4

115g/4oz/¹/₂ cup butter or
   non-hydrogenated margarine, melted
50g/2oz/¹/₄ cup demerara (raw) sugar
   or rapadura
450g/1lb ripe plums, stoned (pitted) and
   thickly sliced
25g/1oz/2 tbsp unrefined caster (superfine)
   sugar or rapadura
30ml/2 tbsp water
1.5ml/¹/₄ tsp ground cinnamon

25g/1oz/¹/₄ cup ground almonds
8–10 large slices of white or wholemeal
   (whole-wheat) bread with the crusts
   sliced off

FOR THE CALVADOS SAUCE
3 egg yolks
40g/1¹/₂oz/3 tbsp unrefined caster
   (superfine) sugar or rapadura
30ml/2 tbsp Calvados

1 Heat the oven to 190°C/375°F/Gas 5. Line the base of four 10cm/4in-diameter, deep, earthenware ramekin dishes with baking parchment. Brush thoroughly with melted butter or margarine. Sprinkle each dish with a little demerara sugar.

2 Place the stoned plum slices in a pan with the caster sugar, water and ground cinnamon and cook gently for 5 minutes, or until the plums have softened slightly. Leave the plums to cool, then stir in the ground almonds.

3 With a plain pastry cutter, cut four rounds out of the bread. Dip the rounds into the melted butter and fit them into the bases of the dishes. Cut four more rounds to fit the tops and set aside. Cut the remaining bread into strips, dip into the melted butter and line the sides of the ramekins completely.

4 Divide the plum mixture among the dishes and level the tops with a spoon. Place the bread rounds on top and brush with the remaining butter. Place on a baking sheet and bake for 25 minutes.

5 Just before the charlottes are ready, whisk the egg yolks and caster sugar in a large bowl until pale. Place the bowl over a pan of simmering water and whisk in the Calvados until very light and frothy. Remove the charlottes from the oven and turn out on to warm serving plates. Pour a little sauce over and around the charlottes, and serve immediately.

Nutritional information per portion: Energy 600kcal/2513kJ; Protein 9.1g; Carbohydrate 69.6g, of which sugars 44.2g; Fat 32.5g, of which saturates 16.5g; Cholesterol 218mg; Calcium 128mg; Fibre 3.1g; Sodium 467mg.

Parsnip cake with orange icing

This fabulous vegan cake is similar to the ever-popular carrot cake, but uses organic non-dairy alternatives to margarine and cream cheese.

SERVES 10

250g/9oz/2¼ cups wholemeal (whole-
   wheat) self-raising (self-rising) flour
15ml/1 tbsp baking powder
5ml/1 tsp ground cinnamon
5ml/1 tsp freshly ground nutmeg
130g/4½oz/9 tbsp vegan margarine
130g/4½oz/scant ½ cup unrefined soft
   light brown sugar or rapadura
250g/9oz parsnips, coarsely grated
1 banana, mashed
finely grated rind and juice of 1 orange

FOR THE TOPPING

225g/8oz/1 cup organic soya
   cream cheese
45ml/3 tbsp unrefined icing
   (confectioners') sugar
juice of 1 small orange
fine strips of orange peel

1 Preheat the oven to 180°C/350°F/Gas 4. Lightly grease and line the base of a 900g/2lb loaf tin (pan).

2 Sift the flour, baking powder and spices into a large bowl. Add any bran remaining in the sieve (strainer).

3 Melt the margarine in a pan, add the sugar and stir until dissolved. Make a well in the flour mixture, then add the melted margarine and sugar. Mix in the parsnips, banana and orange rind and juice. Spoon the mixture into the prepared tin and level the top with the back of a spoon.

4 Bake for 45–50 minutes until a skewer inserted into the centre of the cake comes out clean. Allow the cake to cool slightly before removing from the tin, then transfer to a wire rack to cool completely.

5 To make the topping, beat together the cream cheese, icing sugar, orange juice and strips of orange peel until smooth. Spread evenly over the cake.

Nutritional information per portion: Energy 282kcal/1187kJ; Protein 5g; Carbohydrate 40.3g, of which sugars 22.9g; Fat 11.9g, of which saturates 4.9g; Cholesterol 2mg; Calcium 30mg; Fibre 3.5g; Sodium 108mg.

Country apple cake

This is a great way to take advantage of the season's apple harvest. There are any number of organic apples available nowadays, including heirloom and almost-lost local varieties.

MAKES ONE 18CM/7IN CAKE

115g/4oz/^{1}/$_2$ cup butter or soft
   non-hydrogenated margarine
115g/4oz/^{1}/$_2$ cup unrefined soft light
   brown sugar or rapadura
2 eggs, beaten
115g/4oz/1 cup self-raising (self-rising)
   flour, sifted
50g/2oz/^{1}/$_2$ cup rice flour
5ml/1 tsp baking powder
10ml/2 tsp mixed (apple-pie) spice
1 cooking apple, cored and chopped
115g/4oz/scant 1 cup raisins
about 60ml/4 tbsp milk or soya milk
15g/^{1}/$_2$oz/2 tbsp flaked (sliced) almonds

1 Preheat the oven to 160°C/325°F/Gas 3. Lightly grease and line a deep 18cm/7in round, loose-bottomed cake tin (pan).

2 Cream the butter or margarine and sugar in a mixing bowl. Gradually add the eggs, then fold in the flours, baking powder and spice.

3 Stir in the chopped apple, raisins and enough of the milk to make a soft, dropping consistency.

4 Turn the mixture into the prepared tin and level the surface. Sprinkle the flaked almonds over the top. Bake the cake for 1–1^1/$_4$ hours until risen, firm to the touch and golden brown.

5 Cool the apple cake in the tin for about 10 minutes, then turn out on to a wire rack to cool. Cut into slices when cold. Alternatively, serve the cake warm, in slices, with custard or ice cream. Store the cold cake in an airtight container or wrapped in foil.

Nutritional information per portion: Energy 3810kcal/16031kJ; Protein 35.7g; Carbohydrate 596.6g, of which sugars 451.9g; Fat 159g, of which saturates 68.4g; Cholesterol 260mg; Calcium 617mg; Fibre 16.4g; Sodium 839mg.

Oat and raisin drop scones

Serve these easy-to-make organic scones at tea time or as a dessert – or even a special breakfast or brunch – with real maple syrup or clear honey.

MAKES ABOUT 16

75g/3oz/²/₃ cup self-raising
  (self-rising) flour
2.5ml/¹/₂ tsp baking powder
50g/2oz/scant ¹/₂ cup raisins
25g/1oz/¹/₄ cup fine oatmeal
25g/1oz/2 tbsp unrefined caster
  (superfine) sugar or rapadura
grated rind of 1 orange
2 egg yolks
10g/¹/₄oz/¹/₂ tbsp unsalted (sweet)
  butter or non-hydrogenated
  margarine, melted
200ml/7fl oz/scant 1 cup single (light)
  cream or soya cream
200ml/7fl oz/scant 1 cup water
sunflower oil, for greasing
icing (confectioners') sugar, for dusting

1 Sift the self-raising flour and baking powder together into a large mixing bowl.

2 Add the raisins, oatmeal, sugar and orange rind. Gradually beat in the egg yolks, butter, cream and water to make a creamy batter.

3 Lightly grease and heat a large heavy frying pan or griddle and drop about 30ml/2 tbsp of batter at a time on to the pan or griddle to make six or seven small pancakes.

4 Cook over a moderate heat until bubbles show on the scones' surface, then turn them over and cook for a further 2 minutes until golden.

5 Transfer to a plate and dust with icing sugar. Keep warm while cooking the remaining mixture. Serve warm.

Nutritional information per portion: Energy 3810kcal/16031kJ; Protein 35.7g; Carbohydrate 596.6g, of which sugars 451.9g; Fat 159g, of which saturates 68.4g; Cholesterol 260mg; Calcium 617mg; Fibre 16.4g; Sodium 839mg.

Fruit, nut and seed teabread

Cut into slices and spread with a little butter or non-hydrogenated margarine, with jam or honey, this teabread is an ideal breakfast bread. The dried fruit, nuts and seeds are a fine source of fibre.

MAKES ONE 900G/2LB LOAF

115g/4oz/²/₃ cup dried dates, chopped
115g/4oz/¹/₂ cup dried apricots, chopped
115g/4oz/1 cup sultanas (golden raisins)
115g/4oz/¹/₂ cup unrefined soft light brown sugar or rapadura
225g/8oz/2 cups self-raising (self-rising) flour
5ml/1 tsp baking powder
10ml/2 tsp mixed (apple pie) spice
75g/3oz/³/₄ cup chopped mixed nuts
75g/3oz/³/₄ cup mixed seeds, such as linseed, sunflower and sesame seeds
2 eggs, beaten
150ml/¹/₄ pint/²/₃ cup semi-skimmed (low-fat) milk or soya milk

1 Heat the oven to 180°C/350°F/Gas 4. Lightly grease a 900g/2lb loaf tin (pan). Place the chopped dates and apricots and sultanas in a large mixing bowl and stir in the sugar.

2 In a separate bowl, mix well the flour, baking powder, mixed spice, mixed nuts and seeds. Stir the eggs and milk into the fruit mixture, then add the flour mixture and beat together until well mixed.

3 Spoon the mixture into the prepared tin and level the surface. Bake for about 1 hour until the teabread is firm to the touch and lightly browned.

4 Allow to cool in the tin for a few minutes, then turn out on to a wire rack to cool completely. Serve warm or cold, cut into slices. Wrap the teabread in foil to store.

Nutritional information per portion: Energy 3197kcal/13481kJ; Protein 76.7g; Carbohydrate 518.5g, of which sugars 333.8g; Fat 105g, of which saturates 12.8g; Cholesterol 389mg; Calcium 975mg; Fibre 28.2g; Sodium 275mg.

Caramelized onion and walnut scones

These scones are very good buttered and served with mature Cheddar cheese. Make small scones to use as a base for cocktail savouries, served topped with a little soft organic goat's cheese.

MAKES 10–12

90g/3¹/₂oz/7 tbsp butter or non-
   hydrogenated margarine
15ml/1 tbsp olive oil
1 Spanish onion, chopped
5ml/1 tsp cumin seeds, lightly crushed
200g/7oz/1³/₄ cups self-raising
   (self-rising) flour
5ml/1 tsp baking powder
25g/1oz/¹/₄ cup fine oatmeal
5ml/1 tsp light unrefined muscovado
   (brown) sugar
90g/3¹/₂oz/scant 1 cup chopped walnuts
5ml/1 tsp chopped fresh thyme
120–150ml/4–5fl oz/¹/₂–²/₃ cup
   buttermilk
a little milk or soya milk
sea salt and ground black pepper

1 Melt 15g/¹/₂oz/1 tbsp of the butter with the oil in a small pan and cook the onion gently, covered, for 10–12 minutes. Uncover, then cook gently until it begins to brown.

2 Add half the cumin seeds and increase the heat slightly. Continue to cook, stirring occasionally, until the onion begins to caramelize. Cool. Heat the oven to 200°C/400°F/Gas 6.

3 Sift the flour and baking powder into a large bowl. Add the oatmeal, sugar, 2.5ml/¹/₂ tsp salt and black pepper. Add the remaining butter or margarine and rub in until the mixture resembles fine breadcrumbs.

4 Add the cooked onion and cumin mixture, walnuts and thyme, then bind to make a soft, but not sticky, dough with the buttermilk.

5 Roll or pat out the mixture to an even thickness of just over 1cm/¹/₂in. Stamp out 10–12 scones using a 5–6cm/2–2¹/₂in plain round cutter.

6 Place on a floured baking tray, glaze with the milk and scatter with a little salt and the remaining cumin seeds. Bake for 12–15 minutes until well risen and golden brown. Cool for a few minutes on a wire rack. Serve warm, spread with butter, non-hydrogenated margarine or goat's cheese.

Nutritional information per portion: Energy 131kcal/543kJ; Protein 1.8g; Carbohydrate 3g, of which sugars 1.3g; Fat 12.6g, of which saturates 4.6g; Cholesterol 17mg; Calcium 23mg; Fibre 0.5g; Sodium 51mg.

Hungarian fruit bread

When dried, many of the nutrients and sugars in fruit are concentrated. So too are any pesticide residues. For a healthier choice, always use organic dried fruits for this delightful light bread.

SERVES 8–10

sunflower oil, for greasing

7 egg whites

175g/6oz/scant 1 cup unrefined caster (superfine) sugar or rapadura

115g/4oz/1 cup flaked (sliced) almonds, toasted

115g/4oz/³/₄ cup sultanas (golden raisins)

grated rind of 1 lemon

165g/5¹/₂oz/1¹/₃ cups plain (all-purpose) flour, sifted, plus extra for flouring

75g/3oz/6 tbsp butter or non-hydrogenated margarine, melted

1 Preheat the oven to 180°C/350°F/ Gas 4 and grease and flour a 1kg/2¹/₄lb loaf tin (pan). Whisk the egg whites until they are very stiff, but not crumbly. Fold in the sugar gradually, then the flaked, toasted almonds, sultanas and lemon rind.

2 Fold the flour and butter into the mixture and tip it into the prepared tin. Bake for about 45 minutes until well risen and pale golden brown. Cool for a few minutes in the tin, then turn out and serve warm or cold, in slices.

Nutritional information per portion: Energy 257kcal/1083kJ; Protein 6.8g; Carbohydrate 43.2g, of which sugars 29.4g; Fat 7.5g, of which saturates 0.8g; Cholesterol 3mg; Calcium 74mg; Fibre 1.7g; Sodium 56mg.

Winter

Comforting food is the order of the day this season. Root vegetables such as swede, carrots, turnips and parsnips are all readily available. There are soups, stews and casseroles to warm and nourish, and plenty to delight vegetarians. Fish dishes are flavoursome, while those with a sweet tooth can indulge in a range of fruity and chocolate treats.

Winter farmhouse soup

Root vegetables form the base of this chunky, minestrone-style main meal soup. Always choose organic vegetables and vary according to what you have to hand.

SERVES 4

30ml/2 tbsp olive oil

1 onion, roughly chopped

3 carrots, cut into large chunks

175–200g/6–7oz turnips, in large chunks

about 175g/6oz swede (rutabaga), cut
    into large chunks

400g/14oz can chopped Italian tomatoes

15ml/1 tbsp tomato purée (paste)

5ml/1 tsp dried mixed herbs

5ml/1 tsp dried oregano

50g/2oz dried (bell) peppers, washed and
    thinly sliced (optional)

1.5 litres/2¹/₂ pints/6¹/₄ cups vegetable
    stock or water

50g/2oz/¹/₂ cup dried macaroni

400g/14oz can red kidney beans

30ml/2 tbsp chopped flat leaf parsley

sea salt and ground black pepper

freshly grated Parmesan cheese or
    premium Italian-style vegetarian
    cheese, to serve

1 Heat the olive oil in a large pan, add the onion and cook over a low heat for about 5 minutes until softened. Add the carrot, turnip and swede chunks, canned chopped tomatoes, tomato purée, dried mixed herbs, dried oregano and dried peppers, if using. Stir in a little salt and plenty of pepper to taste.

2 Pour in the vegetable stock or water and bring to the boil. Stir well, cover the pan, then lower the heat and simmer for about 30 minutes, stirring occasionally.

3 Add the pasta to the pan and bring quickly to the boil, stirring. Lower the heat and simmer, uncovered, for about 8 minutes until the pasta is only just tender, or according to the instructions on the packet. Stir frequently.

4 Stir in the rinsed and drained kidney beans. Heat through for 2–3 minutes, remove from the heat and stir in the parsley. Taste the soup for seasoning. Serve hot in warmed soup bowls, with grated cheese handed separately.

Nutritional information per portion: Energy 257kcal/1081kJ; Protein 10.8g; Carbohydrate 39.7g, of which sugars 15.9g; Fat 7.2g, of which saturates 1.1g; Cholesterol 0mg; Calcium 165mg; Fibre 11.4g; Sodium 436mg.

Moroccan spiced mutton soup

Classic North African spices – ginger, turmeric and cinnamon – are combined with chickpeas and organic mutton to make this hearty, warming main-course soup.

SERVES 6

75g/3oz/¹/₂ cup chickpeas,
   soaked overnight
15g/¹/₂oz/1 tbsp butter or 15ml/1 tbsp
   olive oil
225g/8oz mutton, cut into cubes
1 onion, chopped
450g/1lb tomatoes, peeled and chopped
a few celery leaves, chopped
30ml/2 tbsp chopped fresh parsley
15ml/1 tbsp chopped coriander (cilantro)
2.5ml/¹/₂ tsp ground ginger
2.5ml/¹/₂ tsp ground turmeric
5ml/1 tsp ground cinnamon
1.75 litres/3 pints/7¹/₂ cups water
75g/3oz/scant ¹/₂ cup green lentils
75g/3oz/³/₄ cup vermicelli or soup pasta
2 egg yolks
juice of ¹/₂–1 lemon, to taste
sea salt and ground black pepper
fresh coriander (cilantro), to garnish
lemon wedges, to serve

1 Drain the chickpeas and set aside. Heat the butter or oil in a large pan and fry the mutton and onion for 2–3 minutes, stirring, until the mutton is just browned.

2 Add the chopped tomatoes, celery leaves, herbs and spices and season well with ground black pepper. Cook for about 1 minute, then stir in the water and add the green lentils and the soaked, drained and rinsed chickpeas.

3 Slowly bring to the boil and skim the surface to remove the froth. Boil rapidly for 10 minutes, then reduce the heat and simmer very gently for 2 hours, or until the chickpeas are very tender.

4 Season with salt and pepper, then add the vermicelli or soup pasta to the pan and cook for 5–6 minutes until it is just tender. If the soup is very thick at this stage, add a little more water.

5 Beat the egg yolks with the lemon juice and stir into the soup. Immediately remove from the heat and stir until thickened. Pour into warm serving bowls and garnish with plenty of fresh coriander. Serve with lemon wedges.

Nutritional information per portion: Energy 248kcal/1042kJ; Protein 16.3g; Carbohydrate 25.8g, of which sugars 4.1g; Fat 9.5g, of which saturates 4g; Cholesterol 101mg; Calcium 64mg; Fibre 3.6g; Sodium 70mg.

Chicken, leek and celery soup

This makes a substantial main course soup with fresh crusty bread. You will need nothing more than a mixed green salad or fresh winter fruit to follow, such as satsumas, tangerines or apricots.

SERVES 4–6

1.3kg/3lb chicken
1 small head of celery, trimmed
1 onion, coarsely chopped
1 fresh bay leaf
a few fresh parsley stalks
a few fresh tarragon sprigs
2.5 litres/4 pints/10 cups cold water
3 large leeks

65g/2¹/₂oz/5 tbsp butter or 75ml/5 tbsp
    olive oil
2 potatoes, cut into chunks
150ml/¹/₄ pint/²/₃ cup dry white wine
30–45ml/2–3 tbsp single (light) or soya
    cream (optional)
sea salt and ground black pepper
90g/3¹/₂oz pancetta, grilled until crisp,
    to garnish

1 Cut the breasts off the chicken and set aside. Chop the rest of the chicken carcass into 8–10 pieces and place in a large pan or stockpot.

2 Chop 4–5 of the outer sticks of the head of celery and add them to the pan with the coarsely chopped onion. Tie the bay leaf, parsley stalks and tarragon sprigs together to make a bouquet garni and add to the pan. Pour in the cold water to cover the ingredients and bring to the boil. Reduce the heat and cover the pan with a lid, then simmer for 1¹/₂ hours.

3 Remove the chicken from the pan using a slotted spoon and cut off and reserve the meat. Strain the stock through a sieve (strainer), then return it to the cleaned pan and boil rapidly until it has reduced in volume to about 1.5 litres/2¹/₂ pints/6¹/₄ cups.

4 Meanwhile, set about 150g/5oz of the leeks aside. Slice the remaining leeks and the remaining celery, reserving any celery leaves. Chop the celery leaves and set them aside to garnish the soup or reserve a few of the leek pieces.

5 Heat half the butter or oil in a large, heavy pan. Add the sliced leeks and celery, cover and cook over a low heat for about 10 minutes, or until the vegetables are softened but not browned. Add the potatoes, wine and 1.2 litres/2 pints/5 cups of the stock.

6 Season with a little salt and plenty of black pepper, bring to the boil and reduce the heat. Part-cover the pan and simmer the soup for 15–20 minutes, or until the potatoes are cooked.

7 Meanwhile, skin the reserved chicken breasts and cut the flesh into small pieces. Melt the remaining butter or oil in a frying pan, add the chicken and fry for 5–7 minutes until cooked.

8 Thickly slice the reserved leeks, add to the frying pan and cook, stirring occasionally, for a further 3–4 minutes until they are just cooked.

9 Process the soup with the cooked chicken from the stock in a food processor or blender. Taste and adjust the seasoning, and add more stock if the soup is very thick.

10 Stir in the cream, if using, and the chicken and leek mixture. Reheat the soup gently. Serve in warmed bowls. Crumble the pancetta over the soup and sprinkle with the chopped celery leaves or reserved leek slices.

Nutritional information per portion: Energy 253kcal/1056kJ; Protein 16.5g; Carbohydrate 10.3g, of which sugars 2.4g; Fat 14.7g, of which saturates 3.4g; Cholesterol 48mg; Calcium 31mg; Fibre 2g; Sodium 231mg.

Lentil dhal with roasted garlic

This spicy lentil dhal makes a sustaining and comforting meal when served with brown rice or Indian breads and any dry-spiced dish, particularly those with cauliflower or potato.

SERVES 4–6

40g/1½oz/3 tbsp butter or ghee
1 onion, chopped
2 green chillies, seeded and chopped
15ml/1 tbsp chopped fresh root ginger
225g/8oz/1 cup yellow or red lentils
900ml/1½ pints/3¾ cups water
45ml/3 tbsp roasted garlic purée (paste)
5ml/1 tsp ground cumin
5ml/1 tsp ground coriander
200g/7oz tomatoes, peeled and diced
a little lemon juice
sea salt and ground black pepper

30–45ml/2–3 tbsp coriander (cilantro) sprigs,
    to garnish

FOR THE SPICY GARNISH
30ml/2 tbsp sunflower oil
4–5 shallots, sliced
2 garlic cloves, thinly sliced
15g/½oz/1 tbsp butter or ghee
5ml/1 tsp cumin seeds
5ml/1 tsp mustard seeds
3–4 small dried red chillies
8–10 fresh curry leaves

1 Heat the oil in a large, heavy pan. Add the shallots and fry them over a medium heat for 5–10 minutes, stirring occasionally, until crisp and browned. Add the garlic and stir for a moment or two until it colours slightly. Remove from the heat. Remove the shallots and garlic from the pan and set aside.

2 Melt the 40g/½oz/3 tbsp butter or ghee for the dhal in the pan, add the onion, chillies and ginger, and cook for 10 minutes until golden. Stir in the lentils and water, bring to the boil, reduce the heat and part-cover the pan. Simmer, stirring occasionally, for 50–60 minutes until it has the consistency of very thick soup.

3 Stir in the roasted garlic purée, cumin and ground coriander. Season with salt and pepper. Cook for a further 10–15 minutes, uncovered, stirring frequently.

4 Stir in the tomatoes and adjust the seasoning, adding a little lemon juice if necessary.

5 To finish the spicy garnish, melt the butter or ghee in a frying pan. Add the cumin and mustard seeds and fry until the seeds begin to pop. Stir in the dried red chillies and curry leaves, then immediately swirl the mixture into the dhal. Garnish with coriander and the spicy fried shallots and garlic and serve.

Nutritional information per portion: Energy 147kcal/623kJ; Protein 9.3g; Carbohydrate 23g, of which sugars 2.5g; Fat 2.7g, of which saturates 1.4g; Cholesterol 5mg; Calcium 24mg; Fibre 2.3g; Sodium 32mg.

Spiced onion koftas

These delicious Indian onion fritters are made with chickpea flour, otherwise known as gram flour or besan, which has a distinctive nutty flavour. Serve with organic chutney or a yogurt dip.

MAKES 12–15

675g/1¹⁄₂lb onions, halved and
    thinly sliced
5ml/1 tsp sea salt
5ml/1 tsp ground coriander
5ml/1 tsp ground cumin
2.5ml/¹⁄₂ tsp ground turmeric
1–2 green chillies, seeded and
    finely chopped
45ml/3 tbsp chopped fresh
    coriander (cilantro)
90g/3¹⁄₂oz/³⁄₄ cup chickpea flour
2.5ml/¹⁄₂ tsp baking powder
sunflower oil, for deep-frying

TO SERVE
lemon wedges (optional)
fresh coriander sprigs
yogurt and herb dip

1 Toss the onions and salt in a colander. Leave on a plate for 45 minutes, tossing once or twice. Rinse the onions, then squeeze out any excess moisture.

2 Place the onions in a bowl. Add the ground coriander, cumin, turmeric, finely chopped chillies and chopped fresh coriander. Mix well.

3 Add the chickpea flour and baking powder to the onion mixture in the bowl, then use your hand to mix all the ingredients thoroughly.

4 Shape the mixture by hand into 12–15 koftas the size of golf balls. Heat the sunflower oil for deep-frying to 180–190°C/350–375°F, or until a cube of day-old bread browns in 30–45 seconds. Fry the koftas, four to five at a time, until deep golden brown all over.

5 Remove with a slotted spoon and drain each batch on kitchen paper. Keep warm until all the koftas are cooked. Serve the koftas warm with lemon wedges (if using), coriander sprigs and a yogurt and herb dip.

Nutritional information per portion: Energy 207kcal/861kJ; Protein 5.4g; Carbohydrate 19.8g, of which sugars 8.2g; Fat 12.3g, of which saturates 1.4g; Cholesterol 0mg; Calcium 84mg; Fibre 4.3g; Sodium 14mg.

Jerusalem artichokes with garlic

The slightly smoky and earthy flavour of Jerusalem artichokes is excellent with organic garlic, shallots and smoked bacon. These are good with chicken, pork or a classic nut roast.

SERVES 4

50g/2oz/¼ cup butter or 50ml/3½ tbsp
    olive oil
115g/4oz smoked bacon, chopped
800g/1¾lb Jerusalem artichokes
8–12 garlic cloves, peeled
115g/4oz shallots, chopped
75ml/5 tbsp water
30ml/2 tbsp olive oil
25g/1oz/½ cup fresh white or
    wholemeal (whole-wheat)
    breadcrumbs
30–45ml/2–3 tbsp chopped fresh parsley
sea salt and ground black pepper

1 In a heavy frying pan, cook the chopped bacon in half the oil or butter until brown and beginning to crisp. Remove half and set aside.

2 Add the artichokes, garlic and shallots to the pan, and cook, stirring often, until the artichokes and garlic begin to brown slightly.

3 Add salt and pepper and the water. Cover and cook for 8–10 minutes, shaking the pan occasionally. Uncover, increase the heat and cook for 5 minutes until all moisture evaporates and the artichokes are tender.

4 In another frying pan, heat the remaining butter or oil with the 30ml/2 tbsp olive oil. Add the breadcrumbs and fry over a moderate heat, stirring often with a wooden spoon, until crisp and golden. Stir in the chopped parsley and the reserved cooked bacon.

5 Combine the artichokes with the crispy breadcrumb and bacon mixture, mixing well. Season to taste with a little salt and plenty of ground black pepper, if necessary. Transfer to a warmed serving dish and serve immediately.

Nutritional information per portion: Energy 377kcal/1575kJ; Protein 9.3g; Carbohydrate 39.4g, of which sugars 4.5g; Fat 21.3g, of which saturates 9.3g; Cholesterol 42mg; Calcium 31mg; Fibre 2.6g; Sodium 589mg.

Parsnips and chickpeas in garlic, onion, chilli and ginger paste

Organic root vegetables, such as parsnips, often have a knobbly appearance that makes them interesting and individual, and their flavours are sweeter and more intense. The chickpeas will be more tender if cooked without added salt.

SERVES 4

200g/7oz/1 cup dried chickpeas, soaked
 overnight in cold water, then drained
7 garlic cloves, finely chopped
1 small onion, chopped
5cm/2in piece fresh root ginger, chopped
2 green chillies, seeded and finely chopped
450ml/³/₄ pint/2 scant cups plus
 75ml/5 tbsp water
60ml/4 tbsp sunflower oil
5ml/1 tsp cumin seeds
10ml/2 tsp ground coriander seeds
5ml/1 tsp ground turmeric
2.5–5ml/¹/₂–1 tsp chilli powder or
 mild paprika

50g/2oz/¹/₂ cup of ground cashew nuts
250g/9oz tomatoes, peeled and chopped
900g/2lb parsnips, cut into chunks
5ml/1 tsp ground roasted cumin seeds
juice of 1 lime, to taste
sea salt and ground black pepper

TO SERVE
fresh coriander (cilantro) leaves
a few cashew nuts, toasted
natural (plain) yogurt
naan bread or chapatis

1 In a pan, cover the the soaked chickpeas in cold water and bring to the boil. Boil vigorously for 10 minutes, then reduce the heat and boil steadily. Cook for 1–1¹/₂ hours, or until the chickpeas are tender. Drain and set aside.

2 Set aside 10ml/2 tsp of the finely chopped garlic, then blend the remainder in a food processor with the onion, ginger and half the chopped chillies. Add 75ml/5 tbsp water and process to a smooth paste.

3 Heat the oil in a frying pan and cook the cumin seeds for 30 seconds. Stir in the coriander seeds, turmeric, chilli powder or paprika and the ground cashew nuts. Add the ginger paste and cook, stirring frequently, until the water begins to evaporate. Add the tomatoes and stir-fry for 2–3 minutes.

4 Mix in the cooked chickpeas and parsnip chunks with the 450ml/³/₄ pint/scant 2 cups water, a little salt and plenty of black pepper. Bring to the boil, stir, then simmer, uncovered, for 15–20 minutes until the parsnips are completely tender.

5 Reduce the liquid, if necessary, by bringing the sauce to the boil and then boiling fiercely until the sauce is thick. Add the ground roasted cumin with more salt and/or lime juice to taste. Stir in the reserved garlic and green chilli, and cook for a further 1–2 minutes. Scatter the fresh coriander leaves and toasted cashew nuts over and serve straight away with yogurt and warmed naan bread or chapatis.

Nutritional information per portion: Energy 495kcal/2079kJ; Protein 17.9g; Carbohydrate 58.4g, of which sugars 17.6g; Fat 22.8g, of which saturates 4.1g; Cholesterol 0mg; Calcium 185mg; Fibre 16.9g; Sodium 84mg.

Peppers filled with spiced vegetables

Indian spices season the potato and aubergine stuffing in these colourful baked peppers. They are good with brown rice and a lentil dhal. Alternatively, serve them with a salad, Indian breads and a cucumber or mint and yogurt raita.

SERVES 6

6 large evenly shaped red (bell) or yellow
   (bell) peppers
500g/1¼lb waxy potatoes
1 small onion, chopped
4–5 garlic cloves, chopped
5cm/2in piece fresh root ginger, chopped
1–2 fresh green chillies, seeded
   and chopped
105ml/7 tbsp water
90–105ml/6–7 tbsp sunflower oil
1 aubergine (eggplant), diced

10ml/2 tsp cumin seeds
5ml/1 tsp kalonji seeds
2.5ml/½ tsp ground turmeric
5ml/1 tsp ground coriander
5ml/1 tsp ground toasted cumin seeds
pinch of cayenne pepper
about 30ml/2 tbsp lemon juice
sea salt and ground black pepper
30ml/2 tbsp chopped fresh coriander
   (cilantro), to garnish

1 Cut the tops off the red or yellow peppers, and remove and discard the seeds. If necessary, cut a thin slice off the base to make the peppers stand upright.

2 Bring a large pan of lightly salted water to the boil. Add the peppers and cook for 5–6 minutes. Drain and leave them upside down in a colander.

3 Cook the potatoes in lightly salted, boiling water for 10–12 minutes until just tender. Drain, cool and peel, then cut into 1cm/½in dice.

4 Put the onion, garlic, ginger and green chillies in a food processor or blender with 60ml/4 tbsp of the water and process to a purée.

5 Heat 45ml/3 tbsp of the sunflower oil in a large, deep frying pan and cook the diced aubergine, stirring occasionally, until it is evenly browned on all sides. Remove from the pan and set aside. Add another 30ml/2 tbsp of the sunflower oil to the pan, add the diced potatoes and cook until lightly browned on all sides. Remove the potatoes from the pan and set aside.

6 If necessary, add another 15ml/1 tbsp sunflower oil to the pan, then add the cumin and kalonji seeds. Fry briefly until the seeds darken, then add the turmeric, coriander and ground cumin. Cook for 15 seconds. Stir in the onion and garlic purée and fry, scraping the pan with a spatula, until the onions begin to brown.

7 Return the potatoes and aubergine to the pan, season with salt, pepper and 1–2 pinches of cayenne. Add the remaining water and 15ml/1 tbsp lemon juice and then cook, stirring, until the liquid evaporates. Preheat the oven to 190°C/375°F/Gas 5.

8 Fill the peppers with the spiced vegetable mixture and place on a lightly greased baking tray. Brush the peppers with a little oil and bake for 30–35 minutes until they are cooked. Allow to cool a little, then sprinkle with a little more lemon juice, garnish with the coriander and serve.

Nutritional information per portion: Energy 151kcal/633kJ; Protein 3.2g; Carbohydrate 21.2g, of which sugars 8.3g; Fat 6.5g, of which saturates 0.9g; Cholesterol 0mg; Calcium 38mg; Fibre 4.1g; Sodium 17mg.

Mutton shanks with beans and herbs

In this hearty winter dish, full-flavoured organic mutton shanks are slowly cooked in the oven until tender on a bed of tasty cannellini beans and mixed vegetables.

SERVES 4

175g/6oz/1 cup dried cannellini, butter (lima) or haricot (navy) beans, soaked overnight in cold water
150ml/¼ pint/⅔ cup water
45ml/3 tbsp olive oil
4 large mutton shanks, 225g/8oz each
1 large onion, chopped
450g/1lb carrots or swede (rutabaga), cut into thick chunks

2 celery sticks, cut into thick chunks
450g/1lb tomatoes, quartered
250ml/8fl oz/1 cup vegetable or mutton stock
4 fresh rosemary sprigs
2 bay leaves
sea salt and ground black pepper

1 Drain and rinse the soaked cannellini beans and place them in a large pan of unsalted boiling water. Bring back to the boil and boil rapidly for 10 minutes, then drain again.

2 Place the 150ml/¼ pint/⅔ cup water in a large casserole and then add the drained cannellini beans. Preheat the oven to 220°C/425°F/Gas 7.

3 Heat 30ml/2 tbsp of the olive oil in a large frying pan, add the mutton and cook over a high heat, turning occasionally until brown all over. Remove from pan and set aside.

4 Add the remaining oil to the pan, then add the onion, and sauté for 5 minutes until soft and translucent. Add the carrots or swede and celery to the pan and cook for 2–3 minutes. Stir in the quartered tomatoes and the stock, transfer to the casserole and season well with salt and pepper. Add the fresh rosemary and bay leaves and stir again to combine.

5 Place the mutton shanks on top of the beans and vegetables. Cover the casserole and cook in the preheated oven for 30 minutes, or until the liquid is bubbling. Reduce the temperature to 160°C/325°F/Gas 3 and cook for about 1½ hours, or until the meat is tender. Check the seasoning and serve on deep, warmed plates, placing each mutton shank on a bed of beans and vegetables.

Nutritional information per portion: Energy 602kcal/2525kJ; Protein 62.5g; Carbohydrate 33g, of which sugars 13.9g; Fat 25.4g, of which saturates 7.8g; Cholesterol 184mg; Calcium 125mg; Fibre 11.1g; Sodium 178mg.

Steak, mushroom and ale pie

Organic steak has a great quality and fine texture, and is full of flavour – it is delicious in this Anglo-Irish dish. Creamy mashed potatoes or parsley-dressed boiled potatoes and slightly crunchy carrots and green beans or cabbage are perfect accompaniments.

SERVES 4

30ml/2 tbsp olive oil

1 large onion, finely chopped

115g/4oz/1¹/₂ cups chestnut or button (white) mushrooms, halved

900g/2lb lean beef in one piece, such as rump or braising steak

30ml/2 tbsp plain (all-purpose) wholemeal (whole-wheat) flour

45ml/3 tbsp sunflower oil

300ml/¹/₂ pint/1¹/₄ cups stout or brown ale

300ml/¹/₂ pint/1¹/₄ cups beef stock or consommé

500g/1¹/₄lb puff pastry, thawed if frozen

beaten egg, to glaze

sea salt and ground black pepper

steamed organic vegetables, to serve

1 Heat the olive oil in a large, flameproof casserole, add the onion and cook gently, stirring occasionally, for about 5 minutes, or until it is softened but not coloured. Add the halved mushrooms and continue cooking for a further 5 minutes, stirring occasionally.

2 Meanwhile, trim the meat and cut it into 2.5cm/1in cubes. Season the flour and toss the meat in it.

3 Use a slotted spoon to remove the onion mixture from the casserole and set aside. Add and heat the oil, then brown the steak in batches over a high heat to seal in the juices.

4 Replace the vegetables, then stir in the stout or ale and stock or consommé. Bring to the boil, reduce the heat and simmer for about 1 hour, stirring occasionally, or until the meat is tender. Season to taste and transfer to a 1.5 litre/2¹/₂ pint/6¹/₄ cup pie dish. Cover and leave to cool. If you have time, chill the meat filling overnight as this allows the flavour to develop. Preheat the oven to 230°C/450°F/Gas 8.

5 Roll out the pastry in the shape of the dish and about 4cm/1¹/₂in larger all around. Cut a 2.5cm/1in strip from around the edge of the pastry. Brush the rim of the pie dish with water and press the pastry strip onto it. Then brush the pastry rim with beaten egg and cover the pie with the pastry lid. Press the lid firmly in place and then trim the excess pastry from around the edge of the dish.

6 Use the blunt edge of a knife to tap the outside edge of the pastry rim, pressing it down with your finger as you seal the steak and mushroom filling into the dish. (This sealing technique is known as knocking up.)

7 Pinch the outside edge of the pastry between your fingers to flute the edge. Roll out any remaining pastry trimmings and cut out five or six leaf shapes to garnish the centre of the pie. Brush the shapes with a little beaten egg before pressing them lightly in place.

8 Make a hole in the middle of the pie using the point of a sharp knife to allow the steam to escape during cooking. Brush the top carefully with beaten egg and chill for 10 minutes in the refrigerator to rest the pastry.

9 Bake the pie for 15 minutes, then reduce the oven temperature to 200°C/400°F/Gas 6 and bake for a further 15–20 minutes, or until the pastry is risen and golden brown. Serve the pie hot with steamed organic vegetables.

Nutritional information per portion: Energy 1061kcal/4423kJ; Protein 58.8g; Carbohydrate 59.3g, of which sugars 7.6g; Fat 65.3g, of which saturates 24g; Cholesterol 164mg; Calcium 129mg; Fibre 3.2g; Sodium 622mg.

Chocolate mousse with glazed kumquats

Bright orange kumquats balance this rich, dark mousse perfectly. There are some excellent organic chocolates available. It is worth spending a little more on them because they have such a luxurious taste and texture, and good fair-trade values.

SERVES 6

225g/8oz dark (bittersweet) chocolate,
   broken into squares
4 eggs, separated
30ml/2 tbsp brandy
90ml/6 tbsp double (heavy) cream or
   soya cream

FOR THE GLAZED KUMQUATS
275g/10oz kumquats
115g/4oz/generous $\frac{1}{2}$ cup unrefined
   granulated (white) sugar or rapadura
150ml/$\frac{1}{4}$ pint/$\frac{2}{3}$ cup water
15ml/1 tbsp brandy

1 Make the glazed kumquats. Slice the fruit lengthways and place cut side up in a shallow serving dish.

2 Place the sugar in a pan with the water. Heat gently, stirring constantly, until the sugar has dissolved, then bring to the boil and boil rapidly, without stirring, until a golden-brown caramel forms.

3 Remove the pan from the heat and very carefully stir in 60ml/4 tbsp boiling water to dissolve the caramel. Stir in the brandy, then pour the caramel over the kumquats and leave to cool. Once completely cold, cover and chill.

4 Line a shallow 20cm/8in round cake tin (pan) with clear film (plastic wrap). Melt the chocolate in a bowl over a pan of barely simmering water, then remove the bowl from the heat.

5 Add the egg yolks and brandy to the chocolate and beat well, then fold in the cream, mixing well. In another clean bowl, whisk the egg whites until stiff, then gently fold into the chocolate mixture.

6 Pour the mixture into the prepared tin and level the surface with a spatula. Then chill for several hours until it is set.

7 To serve, turn the mousse out on to a plate and cut into slices or wedges. Serve the chocolate mousse on serving plates and spoon some of the glazed kumquats and syrup alongside.

Nutritional information per portion: Energy 431kcal/1805kJ; Protein 6.9g; Carbohydrate 49.8g, of which sugars 49.5g; Fat 22.3g, of which saturates 12.4g; Cholesterol 150mg; Calcium 71mg; Fibre 1.7g; Sodium 56mg.

Christmas ice cream torte

Packed with dried organic fruit and nuts, this torte makes an exciting alternative to traditional Christmas pudding. In fact, it will add flavour to any special occasion.

SERVES 8–10

75g/3oz/³/₄ cup dried cranberries
75g/3oz/scant ¹/₂ cup pitted prunes
50g/2oz/¹/₃ cup sultanas (golden raisins)
175ml/6fl oz/³/₄ cup port
2 pieces preserved stem ginger, chopped
25g/1oz/2 tbsp unsalted (sweet) butter or
   non-hydrogenated margarine
45ml/3 tbsp light muscovado (brown) sugar
90g/3¹/₂oz/scant 2 cups fresh white or
   wholemeal (whole-wheat) breadcrumbs

600ml/1 pint/2¹/₂ cups double (heavy)
   cream or soya cream
30ml/2 tbsp unrefined icing
   (confectioners') sugar
5ml/1 tsp mixed (apple pie) spice
75g/3oz/³/₄ cup brazil nuts, finely chopped
2–3 bay leaf sprigs, egg white, caster
   (superfine) sugar or rapadura and fresh
   cherries, to decorate

1 Quickly process the cranberries, prunes and sultanas in a food processor. Tip them into a bowl and add the port and ginger. Leave for 2 hours.

2 Melt the butter in a frying pan. Add the sugar and heat gently until the sugar dissolves. Tip in the breadcrumbs, stir gently, then fry over a low heat for about 5 minutes until lightly coloured and turning crisp. Leave to cool.

3 Finely process the breadcrumbs in a food processor. Sprinkle a third into an 18cm/7in loose-based springform tin (pan) and freeze. Whip the cream, icing sugar and mixed spice until thick but not yet standing in peaks. Fold in the brazil nuts with the dried fruit mixture and any port that has not been absorbed.

4 Spread a third of the mixture over the breadcrumb base in the tin. Sprinkle with another layer of the breadcrumbs. Repeat the layering, finishing with a layer of the cream mixture. Freeze the torte overnight. Make the sugared bay leaves by painting both sides of the leaves with beaten egg white, dusting evenly with sugar and leaving to dry for 2–3 hours. Chill the torte for about 1 hour before serving, decorated with sugared bay leaves and fresh cherries.

Nutritional information per portion: Energy 504kcal/2098kJ; Protein 6.3g; Carbohydrate 38.4g, of which sugars 21g; Fat 36.4g, of which saturates 17.8g; Cholesterol 61mg; Calcium 92mg; Fibre 2.3g; Sodium 209mg.

Spicy pumpkin and orange bombe

In this fabulous ice cream dessert, the subtle flavour of organic pumpkin is transformed with the addition of citrus fruits and spices. The delicious ice cream mixture is then encased in moist sponge and served with an orange and whole-spice syrup.

SERVES 8

115g/4oz/¹/₂ cup unsalted (sweet) butter or
  non-hydrogenated margarine, softened
115g/4oz/generous ¹/₂ cup unrefined caster
  (superfine) sugar or rapadura
115g/4oz/1 cup self-raising (self-rising) flour
2.5ml/¹/₂ tsp baking powder
2 eggs

FOR THE ICE CREAM
450g/1lb fresh pumpkin, seeded and cubed
1 orange

300g/11oz/scant 1¹/₂ cups unrefined
  granulated (white) sugar or rapadura
300ml/¹/₂ pint /1¹/₄ cups water
2 cinnamon sticks, halved
10ml/2 tsp whole cloves
30ml/2 tbsp orange flower water
300ml/¹/₂ pint/1¹/₄ cups extra thick double
  (heavy) cream or soya cream
2 pieces preserved stem ginger, grated
unrefined icing (confectioners') sugar,
  for dusting

1 Preheat the oven to 180°C/350°F/Gas 4. Grease and line a 450g/1lb loaf tin (pan). Beat the softened butter, caster sugar, flour, baking powder and eggs in a bowl until creamy.

2 Scrape the mixture into the prepared tin, level the surface and bake for 30–35 minutes until firm in the centre. Leave to cool.

3 Make the ice cream. Steam the pumpkin cubes for 15 minutes. Drain and blend to a purée in a food processor. Pare thin strips of rind from the orange; scrape off any white pith, then cut the strips into very fine shreds. Squeeze the orange and set the juice aside. Heat the sugar and water in a small, heavy pan until the sugar dissolves. Bring to the boil and boil rapidly without stirring for 3 minutes.

4 Stir in the orange shreds, juice, cinnamon and cloves. Heat gently for 5 minutes. Strain the syrup, reserving the orange shreds and spices. Measure 300ml/¹/₂ pint/1¹/₄ cups of the syrup and reserve. Return the spices to the remaining syrup and stir in the orange flower water. Cool in a jug (pitcher).

5 Beat the pumpkin purée with 175ml/6fl oz/³/₄ cup of the measured strained syrup until evenly combined. Stir in the cream and ginger. Cut the loaf into 1cm/¹/₂ in slices. Dampen a 1.5 litre/2¹/₂ pint/6¹/₄ cup pudding bowl and line it with clear film (plastic wrap). Pour the remaining strained syrup into a shallow dish.

6 Dip the cake slices briefly in the syrup and use to line the prepared bowl, placing the syrupy coated sides against the bowl. Trim the pieces to fit where necessary, so that the lining is even and any gaps are filled. Chill.

7 Pour the pumpkin mixture into a shallow container and freeze until firm. Scrape the ice cream into the sponge-lined bowl, level the surface and freeze until firm, preferably overnight. Alternatively, churn the pumpkin mixture in an ice cream maker until very thick, then scrape it into the sponge-lined bowl. Level the surface and freeze until firm, preferably overnight.

8 To serve, invert the ice cream on to a serving plate. Lift off the bowl and peel away the clear film. Dust with the icing sugar and serve in wedges with the spiced syrup spooned over.

Nutritional information per portion: Energy 571kcal/2387kJ; Protein 4.2g; Carbohydrate 67g, of which sugars 56.1g; Fat 33.6g, of which saturates 20.5g; Cholesterol 130mg; Calcium 122mg; Fibre 1g; Sodium 168mg.

Dried fruit compote

Compotes made with dried fruit are just as wonderful as those made with fresh fruits, especially in winter when fewer organic fresh fruit varieties are in season.

SERVES 4

225g/8oz/1¹/₃ cups mixed dried fruit
75g/3oz/²/₃ cup dried cherries
75g/3oz/²/₃ cup sultanas (golden raisins)
10 dried prunes
10 dried apricots
hot, freshly brewed fragrant tea, such as
    Earl Grey or jasmine, to cover
15–30ml/1–2 tbsp unrefined caster
    (superfine) sugar or rapadura
¹/₄ lemon, sliced
60ml/4 tbsp brandy

1 Put the mixed dried fruits and the dried cherries in a bowl and pour over the hot tea. Then add sugar to taste and the lemon slices. Cover with a plate, set aside and leave to cool to room temperature.

2 When the fruits are cool, cover the bowl with clear film (plastic wrap) and chill in the refrigerator for at least 2 hours and preferably overnight. Just before serving, pour in the brandy and stir well.

Nutritional information per portion: Energy 189kcal/807kJ; Protein 2.6g; Carbohydrate 46.8g, of which sugars 46.8g; Fat 0.4g, of which saturates 0g; Cholesterol 0mg; Calcium 38mg; Fibre 5.3g; Sodium 20mg.

Orange marmalade chocolate loaf

Do not be alarmed at the amount of cream in this recipe – it's naughty but necessary, and replaces butter to make a deliciously mouthwatering, moist dark chocolate cake.

SERVES 8

115g/4oz dark (bittersweet) chocolate
3 eggs
175g/6oz/scant 1 cup unrefined caster
    (superfine) sugar or rapadura
175ml/6fl oz/³/₄ cup sour cream
200g/7oz/1³/₄ cups self-raising
    (self-rising) flour

FOR THE FILLING AND TOPPING

200g/7oz/²/₃ cup bitter orange
    marmalade
115g/4oz dark (bittersweet) chocolate
60ml/4 tbsp sour cream
shredded orange rind, to decorate

1 Heat the oven to 190°C/375°F/ Gas 5. Lightly grease a 900g/2lb loaf tin (pan) and line the base with baking parchment. Melt pieces of chocolate in a heatproof bowl over hot water.

2 In a separate bowl, beat the eggs and sugar, using a hand-held electric mixer, until thick and creamy. Stir in the sour cream and melted chocolate. Fold in the flour evenly.

3 Pour the mixture into the loaf tin and bake for about 1 hour, or until well risen and firm to the touch. Cool for a few minutes in the tin, then turn out onto a wire rack and let the loaf cool completely.

4 Make the filling. Spoon about two-thirds of the marmalade into a small pan and melt over a low heat. Break the chocolate into pieces. Melt the chocolate in a heatproof bowl placed over hot water. Then stir the chocolate into the marmalade with the sour cream.

5 Slice the cake across into three layers and sandwich back together with about half the marmalade filling. Spread the rest over the top of the cake and leave to set. Spoon the remaining marmalade over the cake and scatter with shredded orange rind, to decorate.

Nutritional information per portion:Energy 475kcal/2004kJ; Protein 7.1g; Carbohydrate 80.1g, of which sugars 60.8g; Fat 16.3g, of which saturates 9.1g; Cholesterol 91mg; Calcium 101mg; Fibre 1.6g; Sodium 56mg.

Orange and nut semolina cake

In Eastern Mediterranean cooking, semolina is used in many desserts. Here, it provides a spongy base for soaking up a deliciously fragrant spicy syrup.

SERVES 10

115g/4oz/¹/₂ cup unsalted (sweet)
    butter or non-hydrogenated
    margarine, softened
115g/4oz/generous ¹/₂ cup unrefined
    caster (superfine) sugar or rapadura
finely grated rind of 1 orange, plus
    30ml/2 tbsp juice
3 eggs
175g/6oz/1 cup semolina
10ml/2 tsp baking powder
115g/4oz/1 cup ground hazelnuts
350g/12oz/1³/₄ cups unrefined caster
    (superfine) sugar or rapadura
2 cinnamon sticks, halved
juice of 1 lemon
60ml/4 tbsp orange flower water
50g/2oz/¹/₂ cup unblanched hazelnuts,
    toasted and chopped
50g/2oz/¹/₂ cup blanched almonds,
    toasted and chopped
shredded rind of 1 orange, to decorate
natural (plain) yogurt, to serve

1 Heat the oven to 220°C/425°F/Gas 7. Grease and line the base of a deep 23cm/9in square solid cake tin (pan).

2 Lightly cream the butter in a large bowl. Add the sugar or rapadura, orange rind and juice, eggs, semolina, baking powder and hazelnuts and beat until smooth.

3 Tip into the tin and level the surface. Bake for 20–25 minutes until firm and golden. Cool in the tin.

4 For the syrup, gently heat the unrefined caster sugar in a small heavy pan with 550ml/18fl oz/2¹/₂ cups water and the cinnamon. Stir occasionally until the sugar dissolves.

5 Bring to the boil and boil fast, without stirring, for 5 minutes. Measure half the boiling syrup and add the lemon juice and orange flower water to it. Pour over the cake. Reserve the remainder of the syrup in the pan.

6 Leave the cake in the tin until the syrup is absorbed, then turn it out on to a plate and cut diagonally into diamond-shaped portions. Scatter with the nuts.

7 Boil the remaining syrup until slightly thickened, then pour it over the cake. Scatter the shredded orange rind over the cake to decorate and serve with natural yogurt.

Nutritional information per portion: Energy 4910kcal/20601kJ; Protein 74.5g; Carbohydrate 638.2g, of which sugars 498g; Fat 247g, of which saturates 74.5g; Cholesterol 816mg; Calcium 738mg; Fibre 18.1g; Sodium 976mg.

Greek fruit and nut pastries

These aromatic sweet pastry crescents are packed with walnuts, which are a really rich source of nutrients. Serve with a cup of organic coffee.

MAKES 16

60ml/4 tbsp clear honey
60ml/4 tbsp strong brewed coffee
75g/3oz/1/2 cup mixed dried
    fruit, chopped
175g/6oz/1 cup walnuts, chopped
1.5ml/1/4 tsp freshly grated nutmeg
milk, to glaze
caster (superfine) sugar or rapadura,
    for sprinkling

FOR THE PASTRY

450g/1lb/4 cups plain (all-purpose) flour
2.5ml/1/2 tsp ground cinnamon
2.5ml/1/2 tsp baking powder
150g/5oz/10 tbsp unsalted (sweet)
    butter or non-hydrogenated margarine
1 egg
120ml/4fl oz/1/2 cup chilled milk or
    soya milk

1 Heat the oven to 180°C/350°F/ Gas 4. To make the pastry, sift the flour, ground cinnamon and baking powder into a bowl. Rub in the butter until the mixture resembles fine breadcrumbs. Make a well in the middle

2 Beat the egg and chilled milk or soya milk together and add to the well in the dry ingredients. Mix to a soft dough, divide into two equal pieces and wrap each in clear film (plastic wrap). Chill for 30 minutes.

3 Meanwhile, to make the filling, mix the honey and coffee. Add the fruit, walnuts and nutmeg. Stir well, cover and leave to soak for at least 20 minutes.

4 Roll out a portion of dough on a lightly floured surface until about 3mm/1/8in thick. Stamp out rounds using a 10cm/4in round cutter.

5 Place a heaped teaspoonful of filling on one side of each round. Brush the edges with a little milk, then fold over and press the edges together to seal. Repeat with the remaining pastry until all the filling is used.

6 Put the pastries on lightly greased baking sheets, brush with milk and sprinkle with caster sugar.

7 Make a steam hole in each with a skewer. Bake for 35 minutes, or until lightly browned. Cool on a wire rack.

Nutritional information per portion: Energy 278kcal/1162kJ; Protein 5g; Carbohydrate 30.2g, of which sugars 8.7g; Fat 16.1g, of which saturates 5.7g; Cholesterol 32mg; Calcium 69mg; Fibre 1.5g; Sodium 80mg.

Baked maple and pecan croissant pudding

This variation of that classic stand-by, the English bread and butter pudding, uses rich, flaky croissants, topped off with a delicious mixture of organic fruit and nuts. Maple syrup-flavoured custard completes this mouthwatering dessert.

SERVES 4

75g/3oz/scant ¹/₂ cup sultanas
   (golden raisins)
45ml/3 tbsp brandy
4 large croissants
50g/2oz/¹/₄ cup butter or non-hydrogenated
   margarine, plus extra for greasing
40g/1¹/₂oz/¹/₃ cup pecan nuts,
   roughly chopped

3 eggs, lightly beaten
300ml/¹/₂ pint/1¹/₄ cups milk or soya milk
150ml/¹/₄ pint/²/₃ cup single (light) cream or
   soya cream
120ml/4fl oz/¹/₂ cup maple syrup
25g/1oz/2 tbsp demerara (raw) sugar
maple syrup and pouring (half-and-half)
   cream or soya cream, to serve (optional)

1 Lightly grease the base and sides of a small, shallow ovenproof dish. Gently warm the sultanas and brandy in a small pan. Leave to stand for 1 hour.

2 Cut the croissants into thick slices and then spread with butter on one side. Arrange the croissant slices butter side uppermost and slightly overlapping in the greased dish. Scatter the brandy-soaked sultanas and the roughly chopped pecan nuts evenly over the buttered croissant slices.

3 In a large bowl, beat the eggs and milk together, then gradually beat in the single or soya cream and maple syrup.

4 Pour the egg custard through a sieve (strainer) over the croissants, fruit and nuts in the dish. Leave the pudding to stand for 30 minutes so that some of the custard is absorbed by the croissants. Preheat the oven to 180°F/350°C/Gas 4.

5 Sprinkle the demerara sugar evenly over the top, then cover the dish with foil. Bake the pudding for 30 minutes, then remove the foil and continue to cook for about 20 minutes, or until the custard is set and the top is golden brown.

6 Leave to cool for 15 minutes. Serve warm with extra maple syrup and a little pouring cream or soya cream, if you like.

Nutritional information per portion: Energy 731kcal/3056kJ; Protein 15g; Carbohydrate 72.3g, of which sugars 49.4g; Fat 45.6g, of which saturates 19.5g; Cholesterol 226mg; Calcium 217mg; Fibre 1.8g; Sodium 507mg.

Orange and coriander brioches

The warm spicy flavour of coriander combines particularly well with organic orange. Serve these little buns with marmalade for a lazy weekend breakfast.

MAKES 12

15g/½oz fresh yeast
225g/8oz/2 cups strong white
    bread flour
2.5ml/½ tsp salt
15ml/1 tbsp unrefined caster (superfine)
    sugar or rapadura
10ml/2 tsp coriander seeds,
    coarsely ground
grated rind of 1 orange
2 eggs, beaten
50g/2oz/¼ cup unsalted (sweet)
    butter or non-hydrogenated
    margarine, melted
1 small egg, beaten, to glaze
shredded orange rind, to decorate
    (optional)
butter, to serve

1 Grease 12 individual brioche tins. Blend the yeast with 25ml/1½ tbsp tepid water in a bowl until smooth. In a mixing bowl, stir together the flour, yeast, salt, sugar, coriander seeds and orange rind. Make a well in the centre, pour in 30ml/2 tbsp hand-hot water, the eggs and melted butter and beat to make a soft dough. Knead on a lightly floured surface for 5 minutes.

2 Return to the clean, lightly oiled bowl, cover with clear film (plastic wrap) and leave in a warm place for 1 hour to double in bulk. Knead briefly on a floured surface and roll into a sausage shape. Cut into 12 pieces. Break off a quarter of each piece and set aside. Shape the larger pieces into balls and place in the tins. With a floured wooden spoon handle, press a hole in each ball. Shape each smaller piece of dough into a little plug and press into the holes.

3 Place the brioche tins on a baking sheet. Cover with lightly oiled clear film and leave in a warm place until the dough rises almost to the top. Heat the oven to 220°C/425°F/Gas 7. Brush with beaten egg and bake for 15 minutes until golden brown. Scatter with orange rind and serve warm with butter.

Nutritional information per portion: Energy 112kcal/471kJ; Protein 2.8g; Carbohydrate 15.9g, of which sugars 1.6g; Fat 4.6g, of which saturates 2.5g; Cholesterol 41mg; Calcium 32mg; Fibre 0.6g; Sodium 119mg.

Moroccan rice pudding

In this simple and delicious alternative to a traditional British rice pudding, the rice is cooked in almond-flavoured milk and delicately flavoured with cinnamon and orange flower water.

SERVES 6

25g/1oz/1/4 cup almonds, chopped
450g/1lb/2 1/4 cups pudding rice
25g/1oz/1/4 cup unrefined icing
    (confectioners') sugar or rapadura
1 cinnamon stick
50g/2oz/1/4 cup butter or
    non-hydrogenated margarine
175ml/6fl oz/3/4 cup milk or soya milk
175ml/6fl oz/3/4 cup single (light) cream
    or soya cream
1.5ml/1/4 tsp almond extract
30ml/2 tbsp orange flower water
toasted flaked (sliced) almonds and
    ground cinnamon, to decorate

1 Finely process the almonds in a food processor or blender with 60ml/ 4 tbsp of very hot water. Push through a sieve (strainer) into a bowl. Return the almonds to the food processor, add a further 60ml/4 tbsp very hot water, and process again. Push the mixture through the sieve into a pan.

2 Add 300ml/1/2 pint/1 1/4 cups water and bring to the boil. Add the rice, icing sugar or rapadura, cinnamon stick, half the butter, half the milk, half the cream and almond extract.

3 Bring to the boil, then simmer, covered, for 30 minutes, adding more milk and cream as the mixture thickens. Continue to cook, stirring, and adding the remaining milk and cream, until thick and creamy. Stir in the orange flower water. Taste for sweetness, adding a little extra sugar, if necessary.

4 Pour into a serving bowl and sprinkle with the toasted almonds. Dot with the remaining butter and dust with a little cinnamon. Serve hot.

Nutritional information per portion: Energy 443kcal/1847kJ; Protein 8.5g; Carbohydrate 66.6g, of which sugars 6.6g; Fat 15.6g, of which saturates 8.4g; Cholesterol 36mg; Calcium 89mg; Fibre 0.3g; Sodium 72mg.

Spiced poached kumquats

Kumquats are at their best just before Christmas. Their spicy-sweet citrus flavour complements both sweet and savoury dishes.

SERVES 6

450g/1lb/4 cups kumquats
115g/4oz/generous 1/2 cup unrefined caster (superfine)
   sugar or rapadura
150ml/1/4 pint/2/3 cup water
1 small cinnamon stick
1 star anise
a bay leaf, to decorate (optional)

1 Cut the kumquats in half and discard the pips. Place the kumquats in a pan with the sugar, water and spices. Cook over a gentle heat, stirring until the sugar has dissolved.

2 Increase the heat, cover the pan and boil the mixture for 8–10 minutes until the kumquats are tender. To bottle the kumquats, spoon them into warm, sterilized jars, seal and label. Decorate the kumquats with a bay leaf before serving, if you like.

COOK'S TIP
Serve these delectable treats with baked ham, roast turkey or venison steaks. They would also make a perfect accompaniment for moist almond or chocolate cake; or serve with organic vanilla or chocolate ice cream.

Nutritional information per portion: Energy 103kcal/441kJ; Protein 0.8g; Carbohydrate 26.6g, of which sugars 26.6g; Fat 0.1g, of which saturates 0g; Cholesterol 0mg; Calcium 33mg; Fibre 0.9g; Sodium 4mg.

Three-fruit marmalade

Seville oranges are the best variety to use for marmalade. They are only available for a short time in winter, so make the most of them.

MAKES 2.25KG/5LB

2 Seville oranges
2 lemons
1 grapefruit
1.75 litres/3 pints/7 1/2 cups water
1.5kg/3 1/4 lb/7 1/2 cups unrefined granulated (white) sugar
croissants, to serve (optional)

1 Halve the fruit, squeeze the juice and pour into a large heavy pan. Tip the pips and pulp into a square of muslin (cheesecloth), gather into a bag, tie tightly with string and tie to the pan handle to dangle in the juice.

2 Cut the skins into thin wedges; discard the membranes and pith. Cut the rinds into slivers and add to the pan with the water. Cook gently for 2 hours until very tender.

3 Remove the muslin bag, squeeze the juice into the pan; discard the bag. Stir the sugar into the pan and heat very gently, stirring occasionally until all the sugar dissolves.

4 Boil vigorously for 10–15 minutes, or until the marmalade reaches 105°C/220°F. Alternatively, pour a small amount on to a chilled saucer. Chill for 2 minutes, then push with your finger; if wrinkles form, it is ready. Cool for 15 minutes. Stir, pour into warm, sterilized jars and cover with waxed paper discs. Seal and label when cold. Store in a cool dark cupboard.

Nutritional information per portion: Energy 6106kcal/26049kJ; Protein 13.2g; Carbohydrate 1612.4g, of which sugars 1612.4g; Fat 0.6g, of which saturates 0g; Cholesterol 0mg; Calcium 1020mg; Fibre 8.9g; Sodium 115mg.

Accompaniments

This chapter contains some classic sauces

and chutneys that add the perfect finishing

touch to satisfying, organic dishes. There

are also tasty breads, such as pumpkin and

walnut, wholemeal sunflower, and cheese

and onion cornbread, which are delicious

with cheeses and cold meats.

San Francisco sourdough bread

Of the many sourdough bread recipes, this organic one is a great place to start. The bread is leavened using a flour and water paste, which ferments with the aid of airborne yeast.

MAKES 2 ROUND LOAVES

FOR THE STARTER
50g/2oz/¹/₂ cup wholemeal (whole-wheat) flour
pinch of ground cumin
15ml/1 tbsp milk or soya milk
15–30ml/1–2 tbsp water

1st Refreshment: 60ml/4 tbsp water
115g/4oz/1 cup strong white bread flour

2nd Refreshment: 60ml/4 tbsp water
115g/4oz/1 cup strong white bread flour

FOR THE BREAD: 1ST REFRESHMENT
75ml/5 tbsp very warm water
75g/3oz/²/₃ cup unbleached plain (all-purpose) flour

2nd Refreshment: 175ml/6fl oz/³/₄ cup lukewarm water
200–225g/7–8oz/1³/₄–2 cups unbleached plain (all-purpose) flour

FOR THE SOURDOUGH
280ml/9fl oz/scant 1¹/₄ cups warm water
500g/1¹/₄lb/5 cups unbleached white bread flour
15ml/1 tbsp sea salt
flour, for dusting
ice cubes, for baking

1 Sift the flour and cumin for the starter into a bowl. Add the milk and enough water for a firm, moist dough. Knead for 6–8 minutes. Return to the bowl, cover with a damp dish towel and leave in a warm place, 24–26°C/75–80°F, for 2 days. When ready, it appears moist and wrinkled and has developed a crust.

2 Pull off the hardened crust and discard. Scoop out the moist centre (about the size of a hazelnut) and place in a clean bowl. Mix in the water for the first refreshment. Gradually add the flour and mix to a dough.

3 Cover with clear film (plastic wrap) and return to a warm place for 1–2 days. Discard the crust and slowly mix in the water for the second refreshment to the starter. Gradually mix in the white flour, cover and leave in a warm place for 8–10 hours.

4 For the bread, mix the sourdough starter with the water for the first refreshment. Gradually mix in the flour to form a firm dough. Knead for 6–8 minutes until firm. Cover with a damp dish towel and leave in a warm place for 8–12 hours, or until doubled in bulk.

5 Gradually mix in the water for the second refreshment, then enough flour to form a soft, smooth elastic dough. Re-cover and leave in a warm place for 8–12 hours. Gradually stir in the water for the sourdough, working in the flour and salt (takes 10–15 minutes). Turn out on to a lightly floured surface and knead until smooth and very elastic. Place in a large lightly oiled bowl, cover with lightly oiled clear film and leave to rise, in a warm place, for 8–12 hours.

6 Divide the dough in half and shape into two round loaves by folding the sides to the centre and sealing. Place seam side up in flour-dusted couronnes bowls or baskets lined with flour-dusted dish towels. Re-cover and leave to rise in a warm place for 4 hours.

7 Heat the oven to 220°C/425°F/Gas 7. Place an empty roasting pan in the bottom of the oven. Dust two baking sheets with flour. Turn out the loaves seam side down on the baking sheets. Cut a criss-cross pattern by slashing the top of the loaves 4–5 times in each direction.

8 Place the baking sheets in the oven and drop the ice cubes into the roasting pan to create steam. Bake the bread for 25 minutes, reduce the oven temperature to 200°C/400°F/Gas 6 and bake for 15–20 minutes, or until it sounds hollow when tapped on the base. Transfer to wire racks to cool.

Nutritional information per portion: Energy 1748kcal/7431kJ; Protein 48.2g; Carbohydrate 398.2g, of which sugars 7.7g; Fat 6.7g, of which saturates 1.1g; Cholesterol 0mg; Calcium 718mg; Fibre 15.9g; Sodium 1489mg.

Pumpkin and walnut bread

Walnuts, nutmeg and pumpkin combine to yield a moist, tangy and slightly sweet bread with an indescribably good flavour. Serve partnered with organic meats or cheese.

MAKES 1 LOAF

500g/1¹/₄lb pumpkin, peeled, seeded and cut into chunks
75g/3oz/6 tbsp caster (superfine) sugar
5ml/1 tsp grated nutmeg
50g/2oz/¹/₄ cup butter, melted
3 eggs, lightly beaten
350g/12oz/3 cups unbleached strong white bread flour
10ml/2 tsp baking powder
2.5ml/¹/₂ tsp sea salt
75g/3oz/³/₄ cup walnuts, chopped

1 Grease and neatly base-line a loaf tin (pan) measuring 21 × 12cm/8¹/₂ × 4¹/₂in. Preheat the oven to 180°C/350°F/Gas 4.

2 Place the pumpkin in a pan, add water to cover by about 5cm/2in, then bring to the boil. Cover, lower the heat and simmer for about 20 minutes, or until the pumpkin is very tender. Drain well, then purée in a food processor or blender. Leave to cool.

3 Place 275g/10oz/1¹/₄ cups of the purée in a large bowl. Add the sugar, nutmeg, melted butter and eggs and mix. Sift the flour, baking powder and salt into a large bowl and make a well in the centre.

4 Add the pumpkin mixture to the centre of the flour and stir until smooth. Mix in the walnuts.

5 Transfer to the prepared tin and bake for 1 hour, or until golden and starting to shrink from the sides of the tin. Turn out on to a wire rack to cool.

Nutritional information per portion: Energy 2663kcal/11186kJ; Protein 66.8g; Carbohydrate 364.1g, of which sugars 94.4g; Fat 114.7g, of which saturates 36.1g; Cholesterol 677mg; Calcium 840mg; Fibre 18.5g; Sodium 1516mg.

Focaccia

This flattish bread from Genoa in Italy is made with flour, olive oil and salt. There are many variations from many regions but this is the traditional type, made with organic ingredients.

**MAKES 1 ROUND
25CM/10IN LOAF**

25g/1oz fresh yeast
400g/14oz/3½ cups unbleached strong
    white bread flour
10ml/2 tsp sea salt
75ml/5 tbsp olive oil
10ml/2 tsp coarse sea salt

1 Dissolve the yeast in 120ml/4fl oz/½ cup warm water. Leave for 10 minutes. Sift the flour into a large bowl, and make a well in the centre. Add the yeast, salt and 30ml/2 tbsp oil. Mix in the flour and add more water to make a dough.

2 Turn out on to a floured work surface and knead the dough until smooth and elastic. Return to the bowl, cover with a cloth and leave to rise in a warm place for 2–2½ hours until doubled in bulk.

3 Knock back the dough, knead for a few minutes, press into an oiled 25cm/10in tart tin (pan) and cover with a damp cloth. Leave to rise for 30 minutes.

4 Heat the oven to 200°C/400°F/Gas 6. Make little dimples all over the dough with your fingers. Pour the remaining oil over the dough, using a pastry brush to take it to the edges. Sprinkle with the salt.

5 Bake for 20–25 minutes until pale gold. Carefully remove from the tin and cool on a rack. The bread is best eaten on the same day, but also freezes well.

Nutritional information per portion: Energy 1661kcal/7020kJ; Protein 37.6g; Carbohydrate 310.8g, of which sugars 6g; Fat 38.2g, of which saturates 5.5g; Cholesterol 0mg; Calcium 561mg; Fibre 12.4g; Sodium 3942mg.

Cheese and onion cornbread

Full of flavour, this tasty organic cornbread is delicious served freshly baked, warm or cold in slices. Either try it on its own or spread with a little butter. It also makes an ideal accompaniment to hot and hearty soups, stews and chillies.

MAKES 1 900G/2LB LOAF

15ml/1 tbsp sunflower oil

1 onion, thinly sliced

175g/6oz/1½ cups cornmeal

75g/3oz/²⁄₃ cup rice flour

25g/1oz/¼ cup soya flour

15ml/1 tbsp baking powder

5ml/1 tsp unrefined caster (superfine) sugar
   or rapadura

5ml/1 tsp sea salt

115g/4oz/1 cup coarsely grated mature
   Cheddar cheese

200ml/7fl oz/scant 1 cup tepid milk or
   soya milk

2 eggs

40g/1½oz/3 tbsp non-hydrogenated
   margarine, melted

1 Preheat the oven to 190°C/375°F/Gas 5. Lightly grease a 900g/2lb loaf tin (pan). Heat the oil in a frying pan, add the onion and cook gently for 10–15 minutes until softened, stirring occasionally. Remove the pan from the heat and set aside to cool.

2 Place the cornmeal, rice flour, soya flour, baking powder, sugar and salt in a large mixing bowl and combine thoroughly. Then stir in the grated cheese, mixing well.

3 In a jug (pitcher), beat together the milk, eggs and melted margarine. Add to the flour mixture and mix well using a wooden spoon.

4 Stir the cooled, cooked onions into the cornmeal mixture and stir well until the onions are evenly incorporated. Spoon the onion mixture into the prepared tin, level the surface and bake for about 30 minutes until the bread has risen and is golden brown.

5 Run a knife around the edge to loosen the loaf. Turn out on to a wire rack to cool slightly and serve warm. Alternatively, leave it on the rack until completely cold, then cut into slices. To store the loaf, wrap it in foil or seal in a plastic bag.

Nutritional information per portion: Energy 1891kcal/7870kJ; Protein 68.3g; Carbohydrate 165.9g, of which sugars 18.3g; Fat 102.7g, of which saturates 52.3g; Cholesterol 589mg; Calcium 1178mg; Fibre 5.2g; Sodium 1302mg.

The organic kitchen

The organic cook can call on a vast array of

ingredients, from fresh fruit and vegetables

to fine-quality meats, poultry, game and

fish. Take the same care with preparation

as you do with selection and storage and

you'll be rewarded with delicious dishes.

This section introduces just some of the

best buys from organic growers and

producers around the world.

Why go organic?

There are many reasons for choosing the organic option, including health, environmental issues, animal welfare, the well-being of farmworkers and fair trade.

What is organic food?

Organic farming is the cultivation of crops and rearing of livestock with natural soil fertility at the heart of the system. For food to be labelled organic, it must be produced according to strict, regulated guidelines.

Organic farmers do not routinely use pesticides, artificial fertilizers, hormones, antibiotics or drug therapies, all of which can have adverse effects on the environment and human health. They promote soil fertility through crop rotation, composting and planting crops that supply specific nutrients, and encourage predator insects such as

ABOVE: *Just some of the fruits available organically: apples, grapes, pineapple, oranges, kiwi fruit and passion fruit.*

ABOVE: *Organic fruit contains more vitamins, minerals and phytonutrients than non-organic fruit. It also tastes better.*

ladybirds (ladybugs) to visit by planting their favourite flowers. They also sometimes introduce other predators to control pests biologically. They also grow crops in polytunnels to keep out insects, thereby avoiding the need for agrochemical pesticides.

Yields from organic and agrochemical farms are now almost identical, with organic yields continuing to grow. Organic farmers also use a wider range of seed banks than agrochemical farmers, selecting the best varieties of crops for their climate and terrain. Organic farming now also utilizes some of the same non-invasive technology as agrochemical farming, such as satellites for predicting weather patterns or mapping insect migrations.

Animal welfare

Organic animals are always free range. By law, their diet is free of genetically modified organisms and solvents. Those that are vegetarian are fed vegetarian food only. Because they have access to the outdoors and are not intensively reared in enclosed spaces, they are less susceptible to disease. Inhumane practices such as battery farming are banned. Dairy cows raised organically have, on average, 50 per cent more room in their barns than non-organic cows and, unlike the latter, they are always provided with bedding. They also enjoy much more time out of doors. The same holds true for organic poultry.

Fish

Organic fish, whether wild or farmed, should come from sustainable fisheries and farms, and be caught using practices that protect the environment. Pollution, insensitive fishing methods and proximity to major shipping lanes all have a detrimental effect on wild fish stocks. The damage from wild and farmed

ABOVE: *These cows are being reared organically, free from hormones that increase milk production or encourage growth.*

salmon interbreeding is immense, with natural fish stocks at ever-increasing risk. Though there is no standard for organics in wild fish, the Marine Stewardship Council offers an accreditation scheme for sustainable wild fisheries. For farmed fish to be labelled organic, they must be reared responsibly. To be sure that your farmed fish is produced responsibly, check that it carries the mark of an organic certification body that you trust.

Wildlife and the environment

Intensive, non-organic farming poses many threats to the environment. Pesticides that target specific pests end up killing or harming many birds and mammals. Organochlorides intended to prevent seeds being eaten have equally damaging effects. Chemicals sprayed on crops and fertilizers penetrate the plants, trickle down into the soil, pollute the land

and drain into the water table before flowing into streams, rivers and lakes, promoting excessive growth of algae, in turn throwing the whole ecosystem out of balance.

By not using these damaging chemicals, organic farmers avoid contributing to this kind of widespread environmental destruction. They also actively promote biodiversity by cherishing hedges, not just for their natural beauty, but also because they play a vital role in providing a habitat for the birds and insects that an organic farm needs in order to function. Organic farmers always keep a strip of wild land around a field because the wild flowers attract butterflies and natural predators that benefit the crop.

Farmworkers' health and fair trade

On agrochemical farms, especially those in developing countries, such as India, protective clothing and

machinery is expensive, while pesticide chemicals are relatively cheap. Consequently, many farmworkers forced to apply these poisons to crops while unprotected are exposed to the risk of various cancers and other illnesses.

By buying organic produce, you can help prevent these types of injustice and go some way towards creating a fairer trading world. Many organic products are fairly traded, which means that a buyer will offer a reasonable price for crops – a principle not generally applied to trade between the developed and developing worlds. For example, a cash-poor farmer may be forced to sell his crop for less than it is worth because he does not have the bargaining power of a multinational organization.

For assurance that an organic product is fairly traded, look out for the Fairtrade seal and consult your supplier or shopkeepers about the goods they sell.

ABOVE: *Organic cauliflower, cabbage, broccoli and Brussels sprouts are high in glucosinolates, which help prevent cancer.*

Alliums

Pungent and strong, alliums are packed with health-giving compounds and impart great flavour to a wealth of dishes. No organic kitchen is complete without them.

Onions, leeks, chives and garlic all owe their characteristic odour and flavour to a compound called allicin. Organic alliums contain more of this compound than their non-organic counterparts, are stronger tasting and have more health benefits. Organic onions are sweeter, while organic garlic is more pungent.

Alliums help to lower cholesterol, have antibacterial qualities and can help to relieve asthma, bronchitis and other sinus and chest ailments.

They also contain cycloallin, an anticoagulant, which helps to protect the heart. The juice from alliums can also be rubbed on to the skin to relieve fungal infections. The

BELOW: *Red onions have been shown to cut cholesterol radically.*

medicinal powers of garlic, the most powerful healer of the alliums, have been recognized for hundreds of years, but all members of the family contain some allicin and have beneficial qualities.

Store all alliums in a cool place and keep them dry or they will begin to sprout. Organic alliums keep as well as non-organic ones.

Onions
Indispensable in the organic kitchen, onions form the basis of innumerable savoury dishes, including salads, stews, soups and gravies. The many varieties include big Spanish onions and small, sweet red onions. Add onions on the side when making an organic cooked breakfast. Not only do they taste delicious with bacon and sausages, but they also cut cholesterol significantly.

Garlic
Both hard- and soft-neck varieties of garlic are on sale in the organic market. Hard-neck garlic, such as Pink Music, has a central woody stem surrounded by five to ten easy-to-peel cloves. It has a richer, more rounded flavour than soft-neck garlic, which is often twisted together, in plaits or braids. Soft-neck garlic, such as Mother of Pearl, has a spicy flavour, each bulb containing seemingly endless smaller cloves. This type can be stored for up to a year, unlike hard-neck garlic, which must be used within six months. Fresh

LEFT: *Garlic contains many nutrients, including flavonoids and vitamin B.*

organic garlic is available but it is at its best when dried and cured. When the thin skin is papery dry, the cloves are mature and will burst with flavour. Always look out for a firm head when buying garlic.

Leeks
A bunch of sweet, young leeks is a bonus in the autumn organic vegetable box. They are good enough to eat raw and taste great lightly steamed or sautéed with garlic.

Spring onions/scallions and chives
These vegetables taste delicious, especially when raw, when they are at their most nutritious. Organic growers often sell bunches of thin, young spring onions, which are delicious in snacks.

ABOVE: *Cooked or raw, sweet baby leeks make a welcome addition to the autumn dinner table.*

Roots and tubers

Organic roots and tubers are much more nutritious and tasty than non-organic varieties. They are best stored unwashed, as a layer of soil helps to seal in the nutrients.

ROOTS
Carrots
Organically grown carrots are high in betacarotene. Try steaming lightly or adding to stews and stir-fries.

Parsnips
When cooked, the flavour of organic parsnips intensifies and they become chewy, with a crunch at the tip.

Swedes/rutabaga and turnips
Organic turnips are delicious lightly steamed and served with fish. They contain calcium and potassium, and are said to soothe aching joints.

BELOW: *Radishes are rich in vitamins and minerals, including vitamins C and B6.*

Beetroot/beets
From yellow mangels to the Italian bull's-eye beet, these are the most colourful root vegetables. Young beetroot tastes very good raw and grated. Alternatively, roast them with other root vegetables.

Radishes
From Japanese daikon to red cherry belle, hot and spicy radishes have high amounts of anti-cancer phytochemicals and also stimulate the gall bladder to manufacture digestive juices.

TUBERS
Potatoes
With organic potatoes, there are two basic textures: waxy, including new potatoes, Pink Fir Apple and Charlotte; and floury, such as Maris Piper and Estima.

Organic potatoes contain vitamin C and the B vitamins. They also support natural immunity and maintain energy levels. The peel can safely be eaten, boosting fibre levels.

Waxy potatoes are ideal for frying and steaming; floury potatoes are good for mashing or creaming.

ABOVE: *Organic farmers produce many varieties of white and red potatoes.*

Jerusalem artichokes
The bitterness of Jerusalem artichokes is caused by cynarine, a powerful liver stimulant that helps detoxify the body. They also help to alleviate rheumatism and arthritis. Try them lightly steamed with fish, or mashed with potatoes and swedes (rutabagas).

Sweet potatoes
Cooked organic sweet potatoes have a smooth gorgeous taste and are rich in vitamins C, E and betacarotene. As they are free of fungicides, you can scrub and bake them whole or steam and mash them like regular potatoes.

Yacon tubers
Almost all yacon tubers are organic and can be eaten cooked or raw. They are a good source of complex carbohydrates, vitamins and minerals. Their crunchy, juicy flesh, sliced or grated, is good in leaf or rice salads. Steamed or roasted, the yacon is even sweeter. They are available through box schemes and at farmers' markets. Store them in the salad drawer.

Squashes and pumpkins

Organic farmers grow many varieties of sweet pumpkins and squashes, from lighter courgettes (zucchini) and marrows (large zucchini) in summer to more heavyweight pumpkins in the winter months.

Courgettes/zucchini and marrows/large zucchini

Organic courgettes range in colour from pale yellow to deep green. They can easily be grown in a garden or on a balcony, and are readily available in stores and farmers' markets. Slice them into salads, or fry with onions, garlic, coriander and paprika for a quick side dish. Marrows are best baked. Try stuffing them with brown rice, almonds, onions and cheese.

Summer squash are effective diuretics and their potassium content helps to relieve high blood pressure.

Pumpkins

Classic round orange pumpkins are full of betacarotene. This has been proven scientifically to help prevent cancer, particularly lung cancer. Pumpkin seeds can be washed, seasoned and roasted for a delicious snack that is rich in protein, minerals and B vitamins. Shell them after roasting to enjoy their full nutty

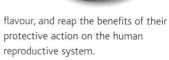

LEFT: As well as betacarotene, pumpkins are a good source of vitamins A, C and E, along with many other essential nutrients.

flavour, and reap the benefits of their protective action on the human reproductive system.

RIGHT: Organic marrows (large zucchini) have a pleasant mild flavour.

LEFT: Courgettes (zucchini) are thought to relieve high blood pressure.

Roasting squash

Cooking squash this way brings out its flavour and retains the goodness.

1 Preheat the oven to 200°C/400°F/ Gas 6. Cut the squash in half, scoop out the seeds and place it cut side down on an oiled baking sheet.

2 Bake for 30 minutes, or until the flesh is soft. Serve in the skin, or remove the flesh and mash with butter and seasoning.

Greens

Organic green-leaf vegetables, such as cabbages, broccoli, chard, Brussels sprouts and cauliflower, are among the best sources of phytochemicals. They help to defend the body against cancer, and should be eaten every day if possible. Leaf vegetables are also a rich source of many vitamins and minerals.

LEFT: *Cabbages contain glutamine, which has anti-inflammatory properties.*

Cauliflowers

When grown organically, cauliflowers are often quite small, around the size of tennis balls. Try to find vegetables that still have their outer leaves. The leaves should be green rather than yellow to indicate freshness, and they are a usable part of the vegetable. Remove them from the cauliflower head and steam for a few minutes.

BELOW: *Organic cauliflowers are often quite small, which was how they looked when they were first cultivated.*

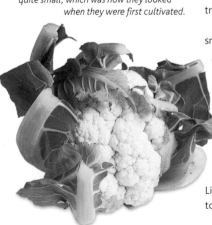

Swiss chard and spinach

Vegetarians and vegans are advised to eat chard and spinach regularly. Swiss chard is a rich, deep green with bright red or creamy white veins, and is almost exclusively found organically grown. Rich in iron, calcium, vitamins A and C and carotenes, Swiss chard is excellent for menstruating women and also as a treatment for anaemia.

Organic spinach is available as small baby salad leaves or fully grown. A superb source of chlorophyll and folic acid, it is an excellent food for preconception and pregnancy.

To prepare, cut chard leaves away from their stems. Steam the stems for two to three minutes, adding the leaves at the end for only a few seconds. Likewise, steam spinach for about 20 to 30 seconds as the delicate leaves

ABOVE: *Spinach is high in folic acid.*

wilt almost immediately. Alternatively, lightly fry the leaves in organic olive oil or butter for a few moments, or simply eat them raw in a salad.

Cabbages

These versatile vegetables come in a variety of organic types, from wrinkly January Kings to smooth purple red cabbages. Some have tight, compact heads, while others are loose leaved. Thinly sliced cabbage makes a very good salad or slaw. Stir-frying cabbage leaves brings out their natural sweetness.

Salad vegetables

Fresh vegetables are at their most nutritious in salads. Most vegetables, except potatoes, can be used raw in salads, and some are particularly suitable.

Lettuces
Organic lettuce is extremely tasty and nutritious. All lettuce contains tiny quantities of opiates, which give it its slightly bitter taste. Organic varieties contain higher levels of phytochemical compounds. Nutritionally, it is best eaten raw, but can also be braised or steamed.

Salad leaves
Pak choi (bok choy), Chinese mustard greens, mizuna and tatsoi are just some organic salad leaves. Lettuces

BELOW: *In addition to vitamins A, B9, C and K, lettuces also contain iron and small amounts of protein.*

and salad leaves grow easily all year round on a windowsill, or outside in spring and autumn. When buying prepared salads, choose only organic. Non-organic varieties are washed in chlorine to prevent the leaves from going brown. Organic prepared salads and ready-cut vegetables are simply preserved by oxygen exclusion and modern refrigeration methods.

Cucumbers
The tiny, plump, almost round lemon cucumber is just one of the many traditional and heirloom varieties grown organically alongside the familiar long, green cucumber.

Watercress and celery
Non-organic watercress and celery are generally treated heavily with pesticides and fertilizers. Agrochemical watercress can be particularly toxic and may contain nitrates. Though smaller, organic watercress is sharper and more

ABOVE: *Fennel contains essential oils that can help combat digestive disorders.*

pungent due to an antibacterial phytonutrient, which is good for bacterial disorders such as food poisoning. It is also believed to protect against – and relieve the symptoms of – lung cancer and skin complaints. Because of its intensity, use in small quantities only in salads or peppery soup with onions, cream and nutmeg.

Celery helps flush excess fluid from the body and relieves constipation. It is great in a mixed vegetable juice or stock. Finely sliced, it adds crunch to a Waldorf salad. Celery is also delicious braised and will add flavour to a stuffing for roast chicken.

Fennel
The aromatic fennel bulb has a very similar texture to celery and is topped with edible feathery fronds. Smaller and tastier than non-organic fennel, organic fennel helps combat digestive complaints such as flatulence. Its distinctive aniseed flavour is most potent when eaten raw in salads. Braised fennel is delicious and sweet. Eat it as soon as possible after purchasing it.

Vegetable fruits

Tomatoes, aubergines (eggplants), (bell) peppers and chillies are treated as vegetables in cooking but are classified botanically as fruit.

ABOVE: *Chadwick tomatoes*

Tomatoes

There is no comparison between the flavour of organic tomatoes and artificially ripened varieties. Tomatoes contain lycopene, which is reputed to protect the body from cancers, especially those of the gastrointestinal tract, breast, cervix and prostate. Lycopene is released when fresh tomatoes are cooked, so products such as tomato purée (paste), canned tomatoes, ketchup and pasteurized tomato juice have higher levels than fresh tomatoes. However, fresh tomatoes are higher in vitamin C, which cooking destroys. Always buy organic tomato products since almost all non-organic prepared tomato products contain genetically modified tomatoes.

Chillies

There are more than 200 different types of chilli, ranging from mild and fruity to intensely fiery. Chillies have antibacterial properties, relieve respiration and chest complaints, and are reputed to strengthen the heart.

The hottest part is the white membrane connecting the seeds to the flesh. Removing it, and the seeds, removes most of the heat. Roasting or grilling (broiling) chillies until charred, and then peeling, moderates the heat and releases the sweetness. Chillies prepared in this way freeze well.

Aubergines/eggplants

There are many varieties of organic aubergines, from the dappled pink Listada de Gandia to the creamy White Sword. To reduce the natural bitterness, slice an aubergine, just sprinkle with salt and leave for an hour. Rinse thoroughly and pat dry before cooking. This also prevents it absorbing excessive oil when frying.

To release their sweetness, simply put on a baking sheet in an oven, preheated to 180°C/350°F/Gas 4,

BELOW: *Serrano chillies contain capsaicin, a phytochemical that is essential for heart health.*

BELOW: *Organic aubergines are meaty and delicious.*

for 30 minutes. Then peel off the skin, chop and serve drizzled with olive oil, tahini and lemon juice. This popular dish is called *baba ganoush*.

Aubergines are also delicious roasted, griddled and puréed into dips.

Avocados

Though high in calories, avocados are packed with essential fatty acids. Unlike non-organic varieties, organic avocados ripen naturally over a longer period. Their creamy flesh relieves PMS, is great for the skin and helps prevent cancer. Slice or cube avocado for salads, or mash with lemon juice and chilli to make guacamole dip.

Peppers/bell peppers

Organic peppers contain vitamin C and capsaicin, which is great for heart health. Green peppers are fully developed but less ripe than other types, and so a little indigestible, though refreshingly juicy and crisp. Orange, red and purple peppers are more mature, have sweeter flesh and are more digestible. To intensify their sweetness, roast or chargrill peppers. They are also delicious served stuffed, sliced into salads or steamed.

Mushrooms

Whether sliced raw in a salad, fried with tamari or soy sauce, or as an ingredient in many dishes, organic mushrooms are certainly tastier than non-organic varieties.

Non-organic mushrooms, and the straw on which they grow, are treated with vast amounts of chemicals, fungicides, insecticides and bleach. Organic mushrooms have no such hazards and are a useful source of B vitamins, potassium, iron and niacin. Organic shiitake mushrooms, prized medicinally for centuries in Japan, are fantastic for the immune system and are a good source of phytochemicals and other nutrients. Dried shiitake mushrooms are readily available in organic stores.

Button (white), cap and flat mushrooms – the most common cultivated variety of mushrooms – are all one type of mushroom in various stages of maturity. Flat mushrooms are good grilled (broiled) or baked on their own or with stuffing.

ABOVE: *Fresh and dried shiitake mushrooms have fantastic benefits for the immune system.*

Chestnut (cremini) mushrooms look similar to button mushrooms but have brown caps and a distinctive nutty flavour.

Intense and richly flavoured, wild field (portabello) mushrooms are ideal for grilling (broiling) and stuffing.

Chanterelles are a pretty yellow colour, with a funnel-shape and a fragrant, delicate flavour. Available dried as well as fresh, they are delicious sautéed, baked or added to sauces.

Store fresh organic mushrooms in paper bags in the refrigerator, and use within a few days of purchase. When you are ready to eat them, wipe the mushrooms gently with damp kitchen paper and trim the stems. Wild mushrooms often harbour grit and dirt and may need to be rinsed briefly under cold running water, but they must be dried thoroughly. Never soak fresh mushrooms or they will become soggy.

Preparing dried shiitake mushrooms
Dried shiitake mushrooms are a useful store-cupboard stand-by. Before they can be used in cooking, however, they must be rehydrated.

1 Quickly wash off any dirt under cold running water, and then soak in tepid water for about 2–3 hours, or overnight. However, if you are short of time, just soak for at least 45 minutes before cooking.

2 Remove from the soaking water and gently squeeze out any excess water. With your fingers or a knife, trim off the stem and slice or chop the caps for cooking. Add the stems to soups or stock. Don't discard the soaking liquid; instead, drain it through muslin (cheesecloth) and use it in soups or stews, or for simmering vegetables.

BELOW: *This mixed selection of organic mushrooms is a useful source of B vitamins, iron, potassium and niacin.*

Peas, beans and corn

These popular organic vegetables can be bought frozen or fresh, so you can enjoy them all year round. They are frozen within hours of being picked and so are still high in nutritional value.

Peas and beans

Organic farmers often rely on legume crops to keep their fields fertile, so there is usually an abundant and varied supply of peas and beans, from sweet mangetouts (snow peas) to meaty broad (fava) beans. Early summer sees the first sweet and tender garden peas, which you can eat straight from the pod. This season is short, but other delights include crisp French (green) beans, sugar snaps and runner (green) beans.

Shelled peas are best eaten lightly steamed or added to sauces and stews in the last few minutes of

BELOW: *Organic mangetouts and sugar snap peas have a fresh flavour.*

cooking. Mangetouts and beans can be sliced raw into salads, stir-fried or lightly steamed as a side dish. Store fresh peas and beans in the refrigerator and use within a week.

Corn

Organic corn cobs are often smaller and paler than their agrochemical

LEFT: *Organic corn cobs have sweet kernels.*

equivalents, but the kernels are beautifully tender and sweet. Corn cobs are best eaten soon after picking, before their sugars convert into starch, the kernels toughen and their flavour fades. Remove the green outer leaves and cook whole or slice off the kernels. Baby corn can be eaten raw or in stir-fries.

One delicious way of serving corn on the cob is to fry it whole in hot olive oil for just a few minutes. The heat will be just enough to release the natural sweetness and caramelize the exterior.

Eda-mame

These are fresh soya beans and they are widely available in Japan and in many parts of the USA. They deliver a complete balance of protein and phytochemicals that are good for maintaining healthy hormone levels.

Preparing eda-mame
This is a good way to appreciate young soya beans in the pod.

1 Separate the pods from the stalks, if they are still attached, and trim off the stem end. Sprinkle the pods generously with salt and rub the salt into the bean pods with your hands. Leave for 15 minutes.

2 Boil plenty of water in a large pan, then add the beans and boil over a high heat for 7–10 minutes, or until the beans are tender but still crunchy. Drain immediately and refresh briefly under running water.

3 Serve the eda-mame hot or cold in a basket or a bowl with drinks. To eat, squeeze the pods with your teeth to push the beans out into your mouth.

Berries and currants

Among the most popular of all fruits are berries and currants, with their glowing colours and delicious sweet, scented juices.

Berries are delicate fruit. Washing them can spoil their texture and flavour. This is just one of the reasons why it is best to buy organic. It is perfectly safe to pop an organic berry into your mouth, whereas the agrochemical fruit will have been heavily sprayed with herbicides, fungicides, insecticides and slug deterrents. Organic berries are smaller and sweeter than non-organic ones.

Strawberries
From organic growers, strawberries are naturally sweet and delicious. Their flavour is concentrated in smaller, less watery fruit. As with all

BELOW: *Organic strawberries*

berries and grapes, they are high in vitamin C. Strawberries are also rich in soluble fibre and betacarotene, and contain phytochemicals that help to ease arthritis.

Blackberries
These high-fibre berries contain a wealth of minerals including iron, magnesium and calcium. They are rich in the bioflavonoids, which act as antioxidants, inhibiting the growth of cancer cells and protecting against cell damage by carcinogens.

BELOW: *Blackberries are a natural and effective antioxidant.*

ABOVE: *Raspberries are high in vitamin C.*

Raspberries
These soft and fragrant berries are effective in removing toxins from the body. To make an uncooked purée or coulis, process some raspberries in a food processor or blender until smooth. Sweeten with maple syrup to taste and add a splash of lemon juice to bring out the flavour. For a smooth purée, press through a nylon strainer.

ABOVE: *Cranberries are a good source of manganese, an essential dietary mineral.*

Store raspberries in the refrigerator for up to two days.

Blueberries
These are exciting considerable interest in terms of cancer research, being rich in anthocyanidins, the phytochemicals that give them their blue colour.

Cranberries
An excellent source of vitamin C, cranberries also provide potassium and vitamin A. Cranberry juice is effective in treating such infections of the urinary tract as cystitis.

Redcurrants
These pretty, delicate berries are rich in antioxidants and carotene as well as vitamins A and C.

BELOW: *Redcurrants*

Grapes, figs and melons

Some of the first fruits ever cultivated, grapes, figs and melons are now available in an enormous range of shapes, colours and sizes. They are excellent sources of essential nutrients.

ABOVE: *Grapes are high in vitamin C and carbohydrates.*

Grapes

There are hundreds of different kinds of organic grapes available, from the largest black sweet varieties through to tiny seedless white ones. Wine grapes are often incredibly fragrant and differ remarkably in taste, texture, size, consistency and acidity. Semillon grapes are a classic variety from south-west France, now grown from Australia to California. They have a delightful, honey-like taste. Sauvignon grapes have herbal and melon flavours, with a citrus fruit edge. Friulian grapes are floral and crisply acidic, whereas Marsanne grapes are relatively low in acidity with a smooth nutty tone to their flavour.

Organic grapes are naturally high in antioxidants. They provide the perfect pick-up for convalescents, being a good source of carbohydrates and vitamin C. Grapes are also easy to eat and taste delicious. Eat them at any time except after a big meal, as they tend to ferment and upset the stomach if it is full. They are best eaten straight off the bunch, or chopped into fruit salads, and taste excellent in fresh green salads.

Figs

The wonderful squashy texture of organic fig flesh is the perfect foil for their crispy seeds, and the delicate fruit has a fantastically sweet and toffee-like flavour. Figs can be eaten raw but are also delicious poached or baked. These fruits are a great cure for constipation and, since they are high in iron, figs can help protect the body against anaemia.

Melons

There are two kinds of melons – musk melons and watermelons. Musk melons include the honeydew and Israeli Ogen varieties. Their flesh is typically sweet and peach coloured. Watermelons include the classic pink-fleshed and deep-green-skinned varieties as well as rare paler versions, such as the Early Moonbeam with its yellow flesh and striped green skin.

Agrochemically grown melons are sprayed with particularly noxious chemicals, including lindane and paraquat. The danger of ingesting these chemicals through a melon's skin is low, as only the inside flesh is eaten. However, if a melon plant is sprayed with pesticides and then watered, some of the agrochemical may be diluted in the water. Melons are storehouses of the water used to irrigate them.

Organic melons are refreshing and cleansing, easing fluid retention and urinary problems. Try serving them cubed on sticks or simply serve a crescent in its skin, decorated with small summer fruits. Melons are also delicious in sweet and savoury salads.

LEFT: *Organically farmed watermelons are filled with the unpolluted water used to irrigate them.*

Citrus fruits

These fruits are enjoyed all over the world. Organic varieties are packed with essential minerals and bioflavonoids.

Oranges, grapefruit, lemons, limes, pomelos, tangerines, satsumas, kumquats and mandarins are all grown organically. Non-organic alternatives are heavily treated with agrochemical toxins – more than 100 different types in US orchards and, potentially, even more in the developing world. Many are also injected with artificial colourings.

The benefits of wax-free citrus peel are obvious to jam makers, with organic marmalade being clearly the best choice. All citrus fruits are great for preventing or treating colds and sore throats, and generally raising immunity levels.

Lemons

Smaller, irregularly shaped organic lemons are juicy and tart. Like all citrus fruits, lemons contain citric

BELOW: *Unwaxed organic lemons*

ABOVE: *Organic oranges are much more flavoursome than non-organic.*

acid but they also work as an alkaline food. Once digested, lemon juice produces potassium carbonate, a neutralizing salt that balances the digestive system.

From soups to sorbets, there is scarcely a dish that does not benefit from a squeeze of lemon juice or a sprinkling of grated rind. A squirt of lemon juice caramelizes and crisps cooked meats, fish and vegetables.

Organic lemons are not dyed and are sometimes greener than agrochemical ones. Ripe lemons will yield to the touch when lightly squeezed. Rolling a lemon firmly over a work surface or in the palms of your hands helps to extract the maximum amount of juice.

Unwaxed, organic lemon rind adds understated warmth to dishes and contributes bacteria-fighting limonine oils. The juice itself is packed with vitamin C and numerous phytochemicals that support the development of general health and a strong immune system.

Oranges and grapefruit

Organic grapefruits are tarter, while oranges are rounder in flavour. Non-organic oranges and grapefruit are routinely coated with anti-fungal waxes that contaminate any dishes prepared with citrus rind or peel. If the skin of the fruit is matt, not shiny, this shows it has not been waxed. Both fruits are high in vitamin C and grapefruits support good gum health. Try squeezing grapefruit juice into a fruit cocktail to add zest, or simply halve the fruit and eat it with a spoon.

Limes

Once considered exotic, limes are now a part of every modern cook's kitchen. The juice is sharper than that of lemons, so use less if you substitute limes for lemons in a recipe.

RIGHT: *Organic limes have now taken their proper place in the organic kitchen.*

Tropical fruit

Though generally smaller than non-organic varieties, organic tropical fruits are denser and sweeter. They are also packed with more essential micronutrients.

Organic tropical fruit should be eaten as soon as it is ripe, as it has a relatively short shelf life.

Mangoes
Rich in vitamin C and carotene, mangoes are reputed to cleanse the blood. For an exotic tropical fruit salad, cube mangoes, papayas, kiwi fruits and pineapple, and drizzle with freshly squeezed orange juice and a little maple syrup.

Kiwi fruits
Packed with potassium, organic kiwi fruits are said to alleviate depression, fatigue and high blood pressure. They contain similar amounts of vitamin C to lemons, and roughly the same amount of fibre as pears. They are smaller and furrier than non-organic kiwi fruit, with darker, less watery flesh.

BELOW: *Mangoes are rich in vitamin C and carotene.*

ABOVE: *Organic dates are naturally sweet and high in energy.*

BELOW: *Pineapples contain an enzyme called bromelain, which is good for the digestive system.*

Papayas
The enzyme papain in papayas cleanses the digestive tract and aids general immunity and health. They also contain vitamin C. The crunchy, spicy papaya seeds add savour and bite to green salads.

Bananas
A major source of potassium, bananas also aid digestion. Ripe bananas can ease constipation and cure diarrhoea.

Pineapples
Organic pineapples have a high enzyme content, one of which, bromelain, deeply cleanses the digestive system, aiding the uptake of all nutritional compounds. Pineapples also contain very high amounts of vitamin C and they are fantastic for the complexion, especially when they are applied to skin topically.

Dates
Organic dates are a rich source of dietary fibre, potassium and folic acid. Naturally sweet, they are great added chopped to fruitcakes and steamed puddings, or you can just eat them whole. They are great energy boosters for athletes, pregnant women and the elderly. They can also be given to children instead of sweets (candies).

Dried fruit
When dried, many of the nutrients in a fruit are concentrated, as are the natural sugars. But, unfortunately, so too are the pesticide residues. Non-organic dried figs not only contain more pesticides weight for weight than fresh figs, but also added fungicides.

Dried apricots are good for eating in the hand, for baking and in jam. They are a rich source of carotenes and, when eaten in quantity, contain useful amounts of vitamin C. Organic dried apricots have also been credited with helping to reduce high blood pressure, protecting against cancer and supporting clear, naturally beautiful skin.

Meat, poultry and game

Organic meat, poultry and game labelled as such by a recognized certifying body is the only real choice for cooks whose criteria are good quality, fine taste and texture, and whose concerns include basic levels of animal welfare.

Beef and veal

Organic beef contains a much better balance of good and bad cholesterol than meat from intensively reared cows because the animals' diet includes a high grass content. Many intensively reared cattle are fed dry food almost exclusively.

For a classic roast beef, use either sirloin or fore rib. Back rib and topside (pot roast) are both excellent slow roasted. When grilling (broiling) or frying steaks, use sirloin, rib eye, rump or fillet steaks. Neck or clod has an open, slightly sticky texture, and is good for stews, whereas shin (shank),

chuck steak and top rump are best for casseroles where whole slices are needed. Pot roast silverside or brisket cuts, as these need to be cooked slowly over a long period. Flank and thin flank are good for making mince (ground beef) for Bolognese sauces and cottage pies. Minced (ground) clod and shin are great for hamburgers and steak tartare because they are virtually fat free. Shin makes a good filling for slow-cooked pies.

If you buy veal, make sure that it is organic. It will not be as pale as intensively farmed veal but it will have come from a calf that has been reared with its mother, not one removed when only a few days old. Veal steaks are best simply pan-fried to seal in their flavour.

Mutton and lamb

Most good supermarkets offer organic lamb, but usually only as chops and mince (ground lamb). Organic lamb is tender and full of flavour. The fat is clearly visible and can be removed easily. Organic mutton can be harder to find but many organic butchers stock it. Minced mutton or lamb, which comes from shoulder, belly or leg meat, can be used instead of minced beef.

Pork

Most organic and non-organic bacon is cured with saltpetre. Although this does help to preserve the pinkish colour of the meat, there are

ABOVE: *Organic lamb is especially tender and full of flavour.*

some concerns about whether this traditional process is entirely healthy.

A few specialist organic and biodynamic pork farms now offer delicious, fine-quality – and darker – pork products without salpetre. High-quality organic pork sausages are also widely available in supermarkets and delicatessens, while traditional organic farmers' markets and delivery services offer an even more extensive range.

Pork is a tender meat, which is suitable for all forms of cooking. Leg is a popular cut for roasting, as is blade, which can be roasted on the bone or boned and stuffed. For a truly succulent roast, try spare rib. Perhaps the most popular cut for roasting is loin, which provides the best crackling. To achieve this, score the fat deeply, rub in salt and roast the joint dry. When grilling (broiling) pork

ABOVE: *Organic beef rib is a healthier choice.*

chops or steaks, it is essential to watch them carefully. They must be cooked through, as underdone pork can cause infection, but they should not be allowed to dry out.

Pork fillet (tenderloin) and schnitzel steaks are the best choice for frying. For braising, choose pork chops, steaks, spare ribs, blade, loin or belly meat. Hand and spring meat is a large cut that can be cubed and cooked in tender pork casseroles and stews.

Chicken, turkey, duck and goose

Organic birds are raised in humane conditions, fed on a natural and (usually) traditional-style diet. Organic poultry is less fatty than intensively reared equivalents because the birds have more freedom to exercise and are not fed growth hormones. Because it is less fatty, the meat benefits from being cooked more slowly.

Organic chicken, duck, goose and turkey are easy to obtain, but goose and turkey tend to be more seasonal dishes strongly associated with Christmas, Easter and Thanksgiving holidays. As well as whole birds, poultry portions and breast fillets are available. They may be on the bone or boneless. Buying whole birds and cutting them up is not difficult, however, and provides the perfect opportunity for making home-made stock.

Organic chicken and turkey need to be cooked slower and longer than non-organic poultry for the best

ABOVE: *Organic turkeys are free to exercise out in the open and are not fed growth hormones. The result is a much tastier, less fatty, more nutritious bird on the dinner table.*

ABOVE: *Barbary ducks are lower in fat than other ducks.*

flavour and texture. Rub the skin with sea salt and different vinegars for added crispness and zest. The stock made from the carcass of an organic bird will be much richer in flavour and colour.

Game

Some game is farmed organically, including rabbit and venison. In some parts of the world, other types of game, such as elk and wild boar, are seasonally available from rural farmers' markets and specialist suppliers. Animals and birds that are truly wild cannot be classified as organic, as their habitat and diet is not controlled and cannot be inspected by an organic certifier. Wild game from areas with low agrochemically managed farmlands is unlikely to be contaminated with chemical pollutants.

BELOW: *Wild boar has a strong taste and little fat.*

Fish and shellfish

Fresh fish is a delicious, healthy and versatile source of protein that can be prepared and cooked very easily. However, as many fish are caught using deeply environmentally insensitive methods, or are raised in unsustainable farms, organic cooks should only ever buy from sustainable farms and fisheries.

Farmed fish

Organic fish farms are clean and humane. Chemicals are used only if infection occurs, not routinely, as in many intensive fish farms. The more fish are crammed into a body of water, the easier the spread of diseases such as furunculosis and parasites like fish lice. Organic fish farmers keep numbers lower, thereby reducing disease and pestilence. Though some non-organic fish farms do maintain healthier numbers,

BELOW: *Pale, organically farmed salmon*

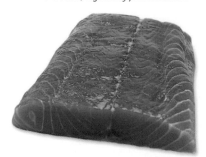

buying organically farmed fish is the best way of being sure that the fish you eat have been well managed.

To be certified organic, fish must be fed fishmeal that is half a by-product of fish for human consumption, and half from sustainable sources. Unfortunately, most fish by-products are from white fish such as cod. Farmed fish, including salmon, do not easily digest this sort of fishmeal, so much can be wasted, only to pollute surrounding waters. Also, white fishmeal has relatively low levels of fatty acids, so organically farmed fish can, in turn, have relatively low levels of Omega-3 oils, unless they are very carefully managed by an expert organic fish farmer. On the plus side, organically farmed fish are not permitted to be fed any genetically modified foods (GM), so buying organic fish is the only way you can be certain that your farmed fish dinner is GM free.

ABOVE: *Seawater fish farms produce excellent sea trout.*

Although good-quality, non-organic salmon usually have relatively low levels of chemical residues, organically farmed salmon have even less and are generally top class in terms of taste and texture.

Salmon, trout and carp taste wonderful grilled (broiled), steamed or fried in olive oil, especially when they are served with a generous squeeze of fresh lemon juice. Smoked in the traditional way, organically farmed fish have incomparable flavour, so different from the bland non-organic product, which is prepared using artificial wood smoke flavouring.

Seawater fish farms

Organic seawater fish farms are beginning to rear many more breeds of fish, including organic sea trout, bass, cod, halibut and bream. As wild fish stocks come under increasing threat, this area of organic farming is set to grow.

The prawn and shrimp industry often replaces rural diverse communities with a single polluting monoculture. To avoid adding to this type of situation, do not buy farmed prawns or shrimps unless they are certified organic.

Shellfish such as cockles, mussels, scallops and oysters are sometimes farmed in enclosures around coastal seawaters. They feed on naturally occurring plankton and are a healthy source of food whose production has a low impact on the environment. Mussels and oysters are also a good source of betaine, a substance that helps to protect against heart attacks. Oysters should simply be prised open with a knife and eaten whole, with a squirt of lemon. To clean mussels, scrub them in fresh water and pull off any fibrous "beards" sprouting between the two halves of the shell. Discard any that are open or fail to snap shut when tapped with a knife.

ABOVE: *Organic mussels and other shellfish are increasingly farmed in enclosures around coastal seawaters.*

Wild fish

There are two basic groups of wild fish: those that live at the bottom of the sea, such as cod, carp, hake, haddock, hoki, Alaskan pollock, plaice, halibut and sole; and those that live in the middle waters or near the surface, including sardines, mackerel, anchovies, pilchards, Atlantic herring and swordfish.

Worldwide, many species of wild sea fish are under threat of extinction for various reasons, not least over-fishing. Also, modern fishing methods and technology – including traps, trawler nets and even radar, planes and submarines – do not discriminate between adults and young fish. Farmed fish often escape and interbreed with wild stocks to produce hybrid mutations, and wild fish are also increasingly subjected to chemical, biological and hormonal attack from polluted rivers and lakes.

To buy responsibly from sustainable sources, look for products from fisheries awarded international Marine Stewardship Council (MSC) certification.

Shellfish

Lobsters and crabs also live at the bottom of the sea but they are only harvested in coastal waters. They are usually collected in pots, either using bait or trapdoors.

Traditionally, scallops and oysters, which also live in coastal waters, are trawled. However, these days they are harvested by divers, which protects the delicate ecosystems found at the bottom of the sea. Other shellfish such as wild cockles and mussels can easily be picked by hand from the bottom of shallower waters.

Currently, however, most commercially available shellfish are farmed. Intensively farmed prawns and shrimps are bad news for organic consumers, so it is best to try to buy wild shellfish. Non-organic shellfish from Iceland – a benchmark country for sustainable fishing techniques – are particularly acceptable as an alternative.

BELOW: *Wild cockles can be picked by hand from the sands at low tide.*

ABOVE: *MSC-certified halibut harvested by methods that protect the seabed.*

Dairy food and eggs

Opting for organic products means obtaining the maximum nutrition – protein and calcium – from whatever dairy foods you eat, without supporting the negative aspects associated with intensive farming methods.

Milk

Organic milk is the only kind of milk guaranteed to be free of genetically modified (GM) ingredients, as many non-organic cows eat GM feed. It is available with varying amounts of cream, from skimmed to full fat. Full-fat (whole) milk generally only contains about 2 per cent fat, so all milk is low-fat food. Although most milk

RIGHT: Goat's, cow's, sheep's and soya milk

is pasteurized, homogenized or sterilized, it can also be found raw. Pasteurization is a heating process that helps to control bacteria levels in the milk. Homogenization distributes the fat content throughout the milk. Sterilization extends the shelf life of sealed cartons so that they do not need refrigeration. These are all permitted under organic certification laws because they do not involve chemicals.

Goat's milk has a distinctive, musky flavour and is easy to digest. Organic sheep's milk is not as pungent as goat's milk, but it does contain more of the lactose that can cause dairy intolerance.

Yogurts, creams and dairy desserts

A natural probiotic, live yogurt boosts quantities of beneficial bacteria in the intestines. This, in turn, aids the absorption of nutrients such as calcium, and offers some protection from various disorders, including tooth decay and heart disease.

Though many of the world's largest non-organic dairy corporations now also offer organic yogurts, creams and dairy desserts, quality can vary. Mass-produced yogurts and dairy desserts are often watery, high in sugar and low in flavour. Whether runny or thick, organic creams should always be mouthwateringly rich. For full flavour, choose products from smaller enterprises that are primarily organic.

Butter

Organic butter tastes richer than non-organic alternatives. Both, however, are equally high in saturated fats, which can raise cholesterol levels and contribute to heart disease. Therefore, it is best saved for the occasional indulgence. That said, it is healthier than many non-organic margarines and spreads, which often contain very damaging hydrogenated or trans fats.

Cheeses

Organic cheeses are made from organic milk, and offer environmental, humanitarian and health benefits. Varieties range from hard types such as Cheddar, Cheshire, Double Gloucester and Lancashire through blues like Stilton and Gorgonzola, to soft and creamy Camembert and cottage cheese. Buying organic cheese is a must if you want to avoid eating genetically modified rennet.

ABOVE: *Organic butter*

BELOW: *Organic Stilton and Brie are widely available.*

Soya milk and other substitutes

Soya beans have been used as dairy alternatives for thousands of years. There are dozens of versions on the market, including the fresh product, which looks like cow's milk but is slightly thicker and has a nutty taste. There is also long-life soya milk, which does not need to be refrigerated until opened, as well as sweetened varieties and versions fortified with extra vitamins and calcium.

Low in calories and with no cholesterol, soya milk is particularly useful for those who cannot tolerate cow's milk. Children who suffer from asthma and eczema often get relief when they switch to a non-dairy alternative such as soya milk.

Soya cream is thicker and richer than soya milk because it is made with more beans.

Other beans can be used in a similar way, as can some nuts and grains. Rice milk is thin and has a delicate taste. Tiger nut milk is similar and sweet tasting. Oat milk is pleasantly mild, while pale yellow pea milk is quite creamy. Non-dairy milks can be bought from health food stores or made at home. Try them on muesli or other organic cereals or in creamy soups. With tea, put non-dairy milk in first and stir the tea thoroughly to prevent curdling. The high acidity in coffee means that curdling is almost inevitable, so best avoid non-dairy milks here.

Eggs

Organic free-range eggs come from hens that have ample access to land free from chemical fertilizers and pesticides. The birds are not routinely debeaked to stop them retaliating when hemmed in by other hens, nor are they given growth promoters. Antibiotics are administered only when unavoidable. It is important to look for labels on eggs that attest to organic certification. Although the term "free range" suggests that hens spend their days out of doors, non-organic free-range birds often have limited access to the open air. Organic eggs are the only eggs that can be guaranteed to be free from yolk colourants.

Look out for other types of eggs at farmers' markets. Duck eggs are a pretty shade of blue, goose eggs are big enough for two, and quail's eggs are small and speckled. They can all be boiled, fried, scrambled or used in cakes, in just the same way as hen's eggs.

When soft-boiled, organic eggs are far less likely to contain the salmonella that is often found in eggs from intensive chicken barns. Soft-boiled or lightly poached eggs have the advantage of containing fewer Cholesterol Oxidation Products (COPS), which means they can be beneficial to blood cholesterol levels.

BELOW: *Organically farmed quail and duck eggs are free from yolk colourants.*

Beans, pulses and soy

These staples provide vital protein for vegetarians and vegans, as well as a range of B vitamins and many essential minerals and amino acids.

BEANS AND PULSES

Most beans and pulses, except lentils, must be soaked overnight before being cooked. Lentils can be cooked straight after rinsing but benefit from an hour's extra soaking. Soaking makes beans and pulses easier to digest, as does cooking them with a small piece of kombu seaweed. Cooking with salt toughens beans, so only season after cooking. Always cook kidney beans thoroughly to neutralize natural toxins. Boil vigorously for 15 minutes, change the water then simmer for about 1¾ hours until tender.

Store beans and pulses in a cool, dry place. Keep packets tightly closed or decant into sealed tubs. Beans and pulses can be kept for years and still be capable of germinating. However, the fresher they are, the better, so buy in small quantities and use quickly.

SOYA BEAN PRODUCTS

Highly nutritious soya bean products, including tofu and tempeh, are ideal for keeping in the refrigerator or freezing. Always buy organic soya products, beause many non-organic soya products are made from genetically modified (GM) beans bred to resist strong pesticides and herbicides. There is no benefit to the consumer in eating GM soya beans; the only advantage is to farmers who can use stronger and stronger chemicals.

Tofu

Also known as bean curd, tofu is derived from soya milk, which is curdled using a natural coagulant. The curds are drained and pressed to make tofu, in a process similar to that used to make soft cheese. Firm tofu can be sliced and fried. It is good in stir-fries, especially when marinated in soy sauce to give it more flavour. For soups, sauces and creamy desserts, use silken tofu. Smoked, marinated and deep-fried tofu are available in health food stores and Oriental stores. Organic tofu can also be bought in long-life cartons.

TVP

Highly processed textured vegetable protein (TVP) is widely used in organic processed foods and is also available dried. It is useful for vegetarian burgers or lasagne, but is low on taste, lacks texture and offers limited nutrition. Fresh soya bean products such as tofu and tempeh are far superior.

Tempeh

This Indonesian food is made by fermenting cooked soya beans with a cultured starter. Tempeh has a meatier, nuttier flavour than tofu and its firmer texture works well in pies. Sliced tempeh taste delicious fried in sunflower oil and tamari or soy sauce and served with pitta bread.

LEFT: Tempeh freezes well, so conveniently keeps for long periods.

ABOVE: Haricot, red kidney, flageolet and pinto beans

Grains

Getting to grips with organic grains is easy. There is a wide selection available, from the many forms of wheat to more unusual grains such as quinoa.

Combining

To get the most protein from non-animal sources, mix grains and proteins. Divide foods into three groups: grains; beans and pulses; and seeds and nuts. In any meal, choose a combination of two of these groups. Baked beans on toast is one classic dish; rice and dhal is another.

Rice

Organic brown rice is tasty, nutritious, easily digested, comforting and satisfying to eat, particularly with fresh stir-fried organic vegetables.

Organic white rice is less nutritious, as most of the minerals and vitamins are lost when the bran and germ are removed in the milling process.

BELOW: *Brown rice contains complex carbohydrates, protein, fibre and B vitamins.*

Bulgur wheat

This pale, sand-coloured grain, made from dried and crushed cooked wheat berries, is nutty in flavour and comes in varying degrees of coarseness. Cook by soaking in double its volume of boiling water for 15–20 minutes. It is usually served cold.

Millet

Organic millet is the only alkaline grain and contains all the essential amino acids. It is a rich source of silicon, which helps build collagen for healthy skin, eyes, nails and arteries.

Quinoa

This tiny, slightly nutty-tasting grain (pronounced "keen-wah") is a good source of protein, fibre and B group vitamins. It is good for stuffings, pilaffs and cereals.

Oats

Organic oats are extraordinarily high in soluble fibre and are excellent for the heart. A bowl of porridge or oat-rich muesli (granola) provides more energy than high-sugar, non-organic breakfast cereals. To make organic oat-based muesli, simply add chopped organic hazelnuts, linseed (flax), sunflower and pumpkin seeds and dried fruit to an oat base. It will keep in an airtight container in a dry cupboard for three months.

Wheat berries

These whole-wheat grains are packed with concentrated goodness and have a sweet, nutty flavour and chewy

ABOVE: *Bulgur wheat*

ABOVE: *Millet*

ABOVE: *Quinoa*

texture. They are particularly delicious in salads, breads and stews, or when combined with rice or other grains. When germinated, the berries sprout into wheatgrass, a powerful detoxifier.

Couscous

This is a form of pasta made by steaming and drying cracked durum wheat. When cooked, it is light and fluffy in texture. A mainstay of Middle Eastern cooking, its fairly bland flavour provides a good foil for spicy dishes.

Flour and pasta

Organic food companies produce many different kinds of milled grains, including buckwheat, rice, rye and maize, while pastas come in all shapes, sizes and colours.

ABOVE: *Spelt flour and grain*

These products have an important part to play in the organic kitchen, particularly for people who wish to eliminate wheat and other high-gluten grains, such as rye, barley and oats, from their diet because they are allergic to gluten. Consult a qualified nutritionist if you have this allergy.

Many of us rely too heavily on wheat for carbohydrates – eating wheat-based cereals for breakfast, sandwiches for lunch, biscuits or cakes for tea and pasta for supper. Rather than cutting out wheat entirely, assess your average daily intake and make sure that you eat a good spread of different organic grains.

Wheat flours and pasta

Depending on the degree of processing, wheat flour may be either wholemeal (whole-wheat) or white. Stoneground wholemeal flour is the best for you since it retains all its valuable nutrients, but white flour is often better in baking. Most pasta and noodles are made of plain durum wheat or wholemeal flour. High in complex carbohydrates, pasta and noodles provide energy over a long period. Wholewheat versions are richer in vitamins, minerals and fibre. There is a wide choice of organic wheat noodles including Japanese udon noodles, thin, white somen noodles, egg noodles and ramen.

Non-wheat flours and pasta

Spelt is one of the most ancient grains and is rich in vitamins and minerals. It is the ancestor to modern wheat, but many people with gluten intolerance are able to digest spelt flour. Flours that do not contain gluten, such as rice, soya, buckwheat, quinoa and millet flours, have different cooking properties. Buckwheat is used

ABOVE: *From back to front, hemp spaghetti, gluten-free corn spaghetti and spiralina tagliatelle*

to make blinis in Russia, soba noodles in Japan and pasta in Italy. Buckwheat pancakes are popular in parts of the USA and France.

Rice flour is used in sticky Asian cakes and sweets, and to thicken sauces. Opaque-white rice noodles are popular in many South-east Asian countries.

BELOW: *Udon noodles are high in complex carbohydrates and will provide energy over a long period.*

Baked goods and other products

All organic breads are better than their non-organic equivalents but some organic loaves are better than others. Find a good supplier whose loaves freeze well, so that you can stock up, if necessary.

Factory-made breads

Alongside some excellent organic factory-made breads, there are some inferior loaves. Factory-made organic bread is sometimes made by the flash-baking method. This uses excessive amounts of yeast to make the dough rise rapidly. These breads have a spongy texture, with mediocre flavour, and are not as nutritional as organic loaves made by hand in the traditional way and allowed to rise slowly. The flash-baking method is cheaper for the manufacturer, but bread made this way is contributing to the current boom in yeast intolerance.

BELOW: *Organic white baguette, wheatfree loaf and naturally leavened campagne (at back)*

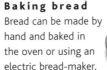

Baking bread

Bread can be made by hand and baked in the oven or using an electric bread-maker, which mixes, kneads, rises and bakes the bread in one easy, hands-free operation.

Wheat is the easiest type of flour to use for conventional yeast-based breads, as it contains plenty of gluten, the sticky substance that keeps dough stretchy and helps it to rise. Use wholemeal (whole-wheat) flour for preference for its fibre content. Quality flours also provide protein and vitamins, especially the B vitamins, and useful amounts of zinc and magnesium, which help to harmonize moods, improve skin condition and promote healing.

Making bread with other flours is more of a challenge, as the gluten content of different grains varies considerably. Rice flour, buckwheat flour, cornmeal and oatmeal, which contain little or no gluten, must be mixed with wheat flour in a yeast loaf, leavened with bicarbonate of soda (baking soda) or used to make flat breads such as rice cakes.

Cakes and biscuits

Commercially baked organic biscuits (cookies) generally contain more vitamins and fewer additives than the non-organic varieties. However, some

ABOVE: *Carrot and raisin cake, gluten-free almond cakes and choc chip hazelnut cookies*

organic sweet products still include too much refined sugar, both in terms of health and taste. So, always check the ingredients list on the packet. Better still, try baking your own. Experiment with the different organic flours on offer, add sweetness by using chopped dried fruit or flavour with grated orange rind, organic cocoa powder or a pinch of cinnamon or mixed spice.

The organic store cupboard
A well-stocked store cupboard is essential for the organic cook. In addition to all the other staple foodstuffs covered in this chapter, specialist organic stockists and farmers' markets are good places to seek out: honey, sugars (such as rapadura, an excellent alternative to refined sugar); maple syrup and sugar; fruit syrups and pastes; cocoa and chocolate; jams, marmalades, pickles and preserves; nuts and seeds; and organic cooking oils such as olive oil and various nut oils, along with cold-pressed sunflower and safflower oils.

Index